Christians in Egypt

Christians in Egypt

Orthodox, Catholic, and Protestant Communities Past and Present

Otto F. A. Meinardus

The American University in Cairo Press

Cairo New York

The publisher would like to thank Dr. Cornelis Hulsman and Dr. David Grafton for their valuable help in the final editing stages of this book, following the death of Dr. Meinardus in September 2005.

The American University in Cairo Press
113 Sharia Kasr el Aini, Cairo, Egypt
420 Fifth Avenue, New York, NY 10018
www.aucpress.com

Part of chapter 1 originally appeared in a different form in *Coptologia* 19 (2003) and is reproduced by permission.
Part of chapter 3 and the Postscript originally appeared in a different form in the *Coptic Church Review* 18/3 (1997) and 20/4 (1999), and are reproduced by permission.
Part of chapter 3 originally appeared in a different form in *Ostkirchliche Studien* XIV (1965), pp. 305–26, as "The Mission of Peter Heyling of Lübeck," and is reproduced by permission.

Dar el Kutub No. 14096/05
ISBN 978 977 424 973 0

2 3 4 5 6 7 8 9 10 11 12 12 11 10 09 08 07

Designed by Joanne Cunningham/AUC Press Design Center
Printed in Egypt

Contents

Preface

Christians in Egypt is the final part of a trilogy on Egyptian Christianity. *Two Thousand Years of Coptic Christianity* (Cairo: The American University in Cairo Press, 1999) provided a comprehensive presentation of the history, traditions, theology, and structures of the Coptic Orthodox Church from its beginnings through to the twenty-first century. *Coptic Saints and Pilgrimages* (Cairo: The American University in Cairo Press, 2002) reflected the spirituality, the lives of the saints, and the popular piety of the Copts with their manifold institutions. The present volume responds to a deficit in our knowledge of the wide spectrum of the various forms of Christianity in Egypt. Interfaith conferences and ecumenical studies have shown that many faithful Christians of a given Orthodox, Catholic, or Evangelical church have a solid and profound knowledge of their own community, yet are often uninformed and ignorant of the faith, customs, and practices of other Christian denominations. Recent developments among Christian communities in Egypt have provided many situations in which ignorance and obstinacy have led to unfortunate prejudices, thereby poisoning the religious climate among Christians in a non-Christian environment. For this reason alone it is to be hoped that an additional effect of this book will be to lead toward a more mature mutual understanding. The purpose of this book is to present a compilation of the principal Christian churches and organizations in Egypt without specific references to doctrinal or spiritual values. Therefore, the traditional issues pertaining to orthodoxy, heterodoxy, or heresies are omitted intentionally. In many ways, the chapters of this volume ought to be seen as an updating of some of the information that I published some forty years ago. I collected material on churches and organizations in Egypt during 2004/5, realizing though that by 2006, some of this information might already be considered 'church history.'

In the process of compiling the data for this volume I depended upon the helpful cooperation of Dr. Cornelis Hulsman of *Arab-West* Report, Dr. David Grafton, Dr. Christiaan van Nispen, and Dr. Ashraf Salama. I am very grateful to them for all their help and support.

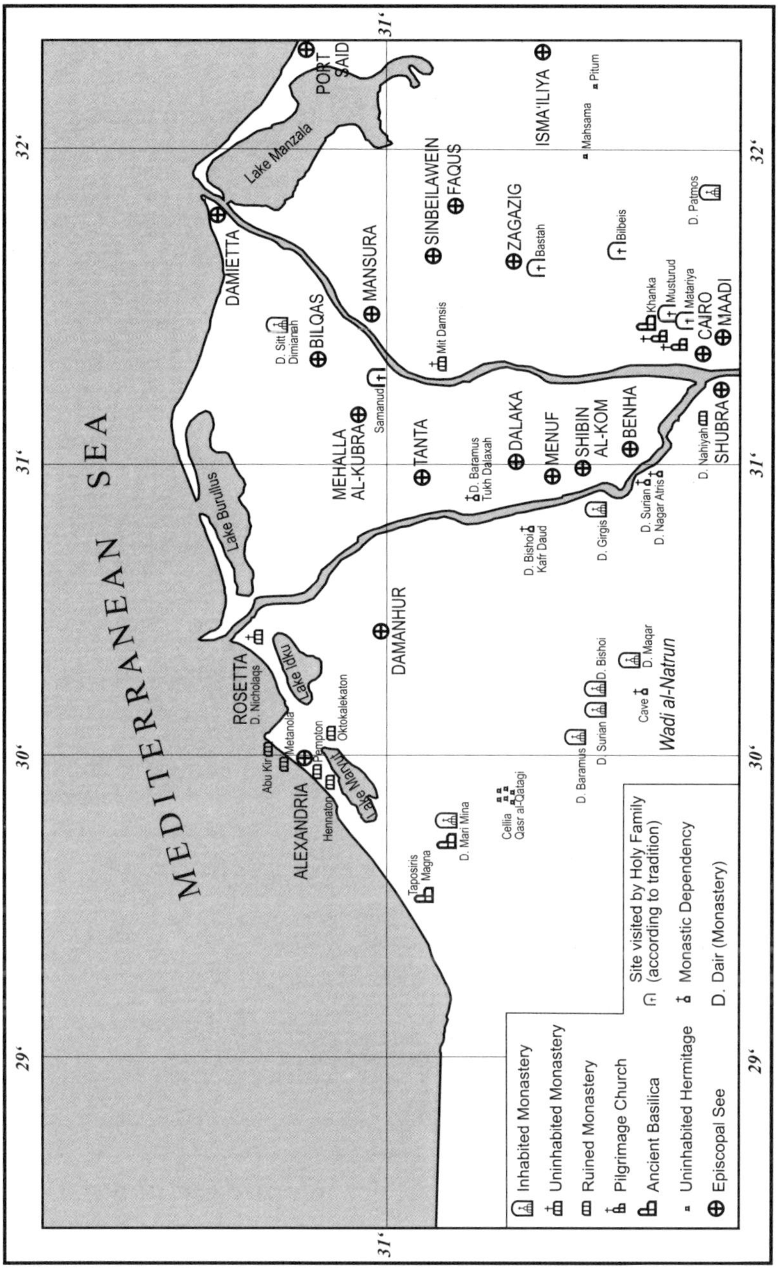

Coptic Orthodox Dioceses
Nile Delta

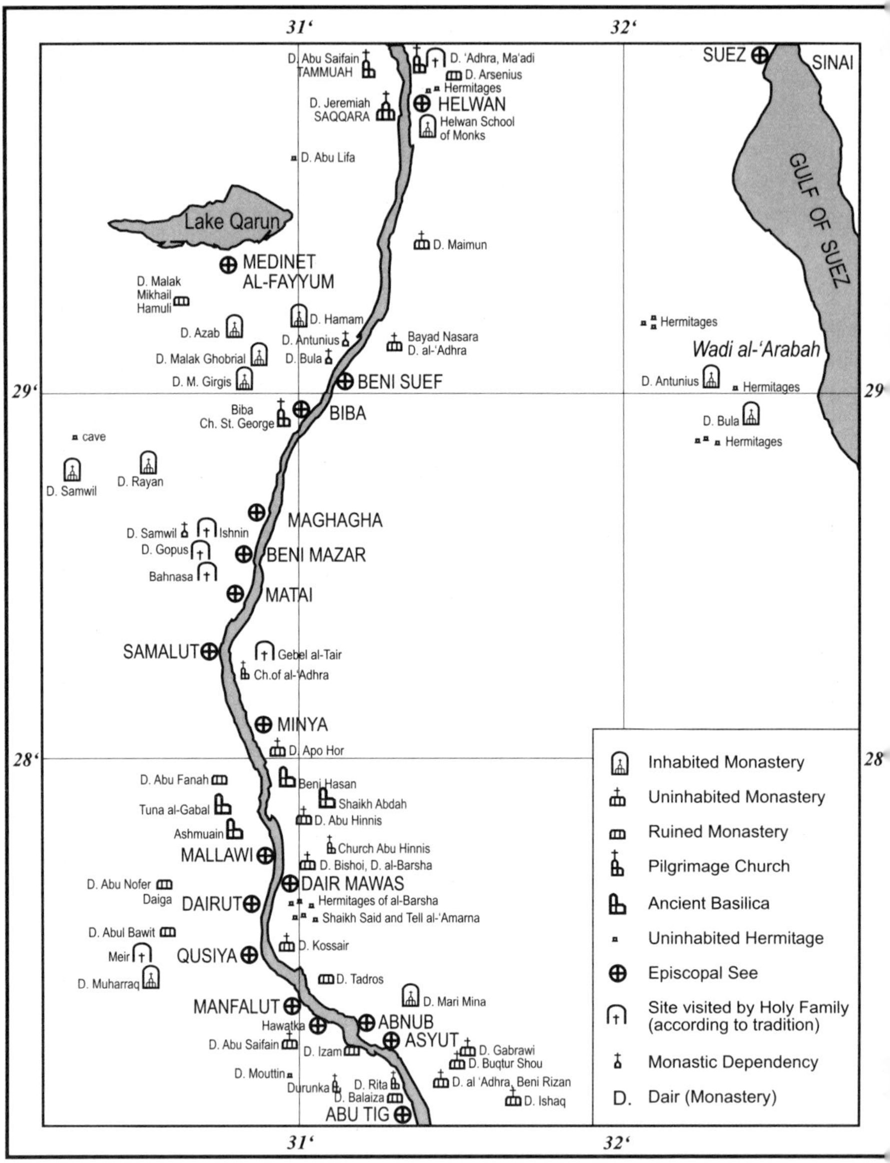

Coptic Orthodox Dioceses
Upper Egypt (north)

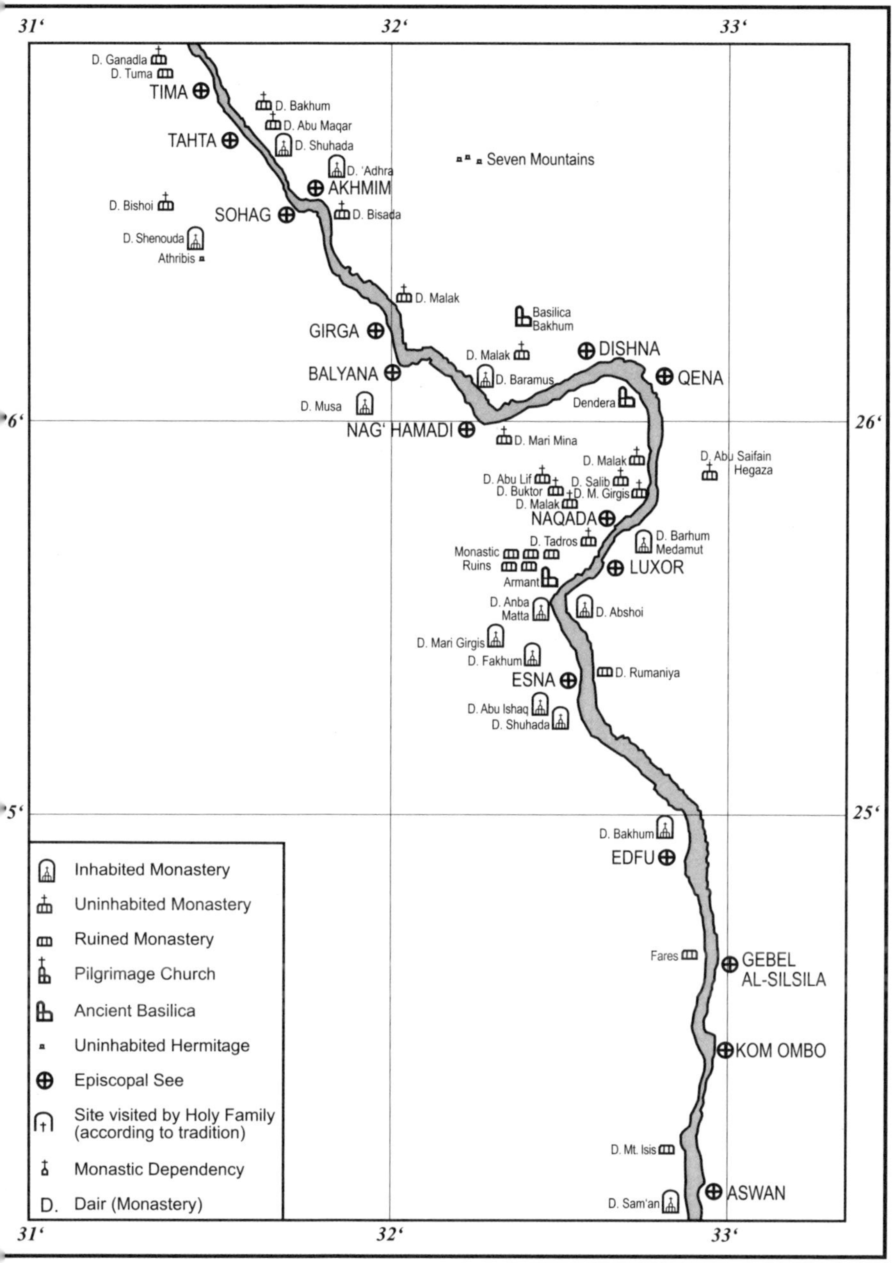

Coptic Orthodox Dioceses
Upper Egypt (south)

1

Egyptian Christians as Heirs of a Pharaonic Heritage

During the past one hundred years, numerous anthropologists, Egyptologists, and theologians have demonstrated the influence of the manners and customs of the ancient Egyptians upon their Christian sons and daughters. To demonstrate this, five altogether different aspects of Egyptian life have been selected and will be outlined below.

Pharaonic Survival, Similarities, Resemblances, and Disparities

In Lawrence Durrell's famous *Alexandria Quartet*, the Copt Narouz engages his British friend Mountolive in a lengthy discussion about his religious and ethnic ancestors. "'Do you know what the Muslims call us?' he asks. 'I will tell you, '*Gins Pharaoony*.' Yes, we are *genus Pharaonicus*, the true descendants of the ancients, the true marrow of Egypt. . . . We are Christians like you, only of the oldest and purest strain. . . .'"[1]

In his preface to the *Coptic Encyclopedia*, Professor Aziz S. Atiya clearly stated that the Copts are the purest descendants and heirs of the ancient Egyptians. To this day, many Copts insist that they are the true sons and daughters of the pharaohs, the historic era in which the country was neither ruled nor looted nor despoiled by foreign masters. Young Coptic women take pride in their classical pharaonic physiognomy, the ideal being the famous limestone bust of the Berlin Nefertiti, the wife of Akhenaten. Young Copts experience a kind of self-confidence and self-assurance realizing that they are heirs of the great pharaohs of the New Kingdom, be it Thutmosis III or Ramesses II. To this day, Egyptian Christians are named after their pre-Christian ancestors: Amonius, Anub, Bakhum, Isis, Shenuda, Serapion, Ramses, Wissa. The present religious and cultural renaissance of the Copts is also filled with reminiscences of their distinguished pharaonic heritage.

Much has been written about pharaonic and pre-Christian survivals in the theology and piety of the Copts. For many centuries the Christians of the Nile Valley had shared rather conflicting ideas and attitudes toward their ancestors. Visitors to the pharaonic tombs and temples on either side of the Nile Valley are often surprised and shocked about the wanton and disgraceful destruction of paintings and reliefs of pre-Christian deities by iconoclastic monks. In order to demonstrate their aversion to and repugnance of pre-Christian paganism, they scratched out the eyes of the gods and defaced the paintings, erasing their representations.

There were, however, a few pre-Christian elements which the Copts adopted. These they readily infused into their Judaeo-Hellenistic religiosity. A definite and clear cult-transfer was the adoption of the pharaonic *ankh*, the 'key of life.' The pre-Christian gods presented this life-bestowing symbol to the pharaoh, thereby transferring to him the 'divine spirit.' With this ceremony, the pharaoh was made 'a son of god,' a representative of the deity on earth. For the early Christians the adoption of the cross appeared as a problem. Neither the Hebrew Old Testament, nor the Greek Septuagint, mention the word 'cross,' since crucifixion as a form of capital punishment did not exist among Semitic peoples. The Apostle Paul clearly stated that the cross was "a stumbling-block to the Jews and folly to the Gentiles" (1 Corinthians 1:23). For the Christians, however, the symbol of reconciliation with God (Ephesians 1:16). In the Synoptic Gospels, Jesus referred to taking one's cross and following him as a demand for discipleship (Mt 10:38).

It was during the fifth century that the Egyptian Christians adopted the pharaonic hieroglyph for life as their symbol to express their belief in the life eternal. It was probably the theologian Rufinus of Aquileia (fifth century) who first saw in the pre-Christian *crux ansata*, the symbol of Christ's redemptive cross. Following the destruction of the Serapeum of Alexandria by the Coptic patriarch Theophilus (385–412), Socrates Scholasticus writes: "The Christians maintain that the cross is the symbol of Christ's redeeming death, a sign that belongs to them." From the sixth century, especially in Upper Egypt, the cross may be fund on stelae, tombstones, and textiles.[2]

Repeatedly, theologians, and Egyptologists have referred to certain similarities of content in the Psalm 104 and the Hymn of Aten. However, it is very doubtful that the Coptic monks, while reciting the Psalm 104, were aware of resemblances between the biblical poem of creation and God's control over nature, and Akhnaten's Hymn to the sun as the source of life. The parallels between the two hymns of praise may possibly be due to some acquaintance on the part of the psalmist with the Egyptian poem, yet the differences between the two hymns of praise are actually more notable than their similarities. In the Egyptian poem the sun is the creator, whereas in the Hebrew psalm the sun is part of the handiwork of the Lord.

Also, with respect to the Athanasian doctrine of the Holy Trinity, suggestions were made regarding certain theological similarities with the Egyptian pantheon. Indeed, it appears very doubtful that the fourth-century Alexandrian theologians and their successors ever thought of the various pre-Christian Egyptian triads when they incorporated the biblical personae into their statement of faith. Neither the Theban Amun, Mut, and Khons; the Memphitic Ptah, Sekhmet, and Nefertum; or the Edfuan Horus, Hathor, and Harsomthus are comparable to the theological structures of the fourth-century doctrine of the Holy Trinity.

An interesting relationship of a pre-Christian cult to the piety of the early Nile Valley Christians is found in the collections of terra-cotta lamps with reliefs of a frog, a symbol which the Christians interpreted as signifying life and the resurrection. An Egyptian terra-cotta lamp with the frog design in the Museum of Turin has the inscription "I am the resurrection," while similar lamps with the symbol of the cross are found in several museums.

Ever since the Middle Ages, the equestrian military saints have played an important role in the hagiology and iconography of the Copts. Hundreds of churches and altars are dedicated to Sts. George, Theodore, Mercurius, Menas, Iskhirun, and others. It has been maintained that the Coptic veneration of these saints defeating and overcoming the personification of evil are a Christian version of the well-known story of Bellerophon on his Pegasus killing the Chimera, that strange cross-breed of lion, goat, and serpent. The myth of Bellerophon and the Chimera was well known among the early Christians. A sixth-century linen textile from Antinoë depicts the royal son on his flying horse conquering a chimera in its orbiculus. The same theme is also presented in the fourth/fifth-century Upper Egyptian sandstone figure of the equestrian Horus spearing a crocodile. In all these cases, universal archetypical models demonstrate the heroic conquest of the "righteous" person over the threats of destruction.

Visitors to the Coptic Museum in Old Cairo are often fascinated by the fifth-century wall paintings of the Maria Lactans, the Virgin suckling the Christ child, in the prayer-niches of the Upper Egyptian monasteries. Only a few feet away, there are several limestone representations of Isis giving her breast to her son Horus or the fertility goddess Renenutet nursing the agricultural deity Neper. The similaries are striking and in many ways remarkable. However, the suckling godmother is one of those universal archetypes. There is Aphrodite holding the youthful Eros in her arms, the young Zeus stretching toward the breast of Rhea, or the famous Venus Genetrix holding the babe in swaddling clothes. Throughout the ages, there were the Egyptian mothers suckling their children, a common and everyday sight in the villages and towns of the Nile Valley that may well have inspired the piety of the Copts to portray their Mother of God as the milk-dispersing Virgin, the Galactotrophousa.

Dreams for Healing and for Ascertaining the Truth

For the Ancient Egyptian, the analysis of dreams was often employed for diagnostic purposes in the therapeutical process of patients suffering from a wide spectrum of diseases. The incubation centers in the temples of Dendera, the famous temple of Hatshepsut in Dair al-Bahari, or the Serapea of Memphis and Canopus were well known throughout the ancient world. They fulfilled similar therapeutical functions as the asclepiad of Epidaurus, Pergamon, and Cos.

The biblical dreams of the pharaoh and his domestic staff which were interpreted by Joseph are well known (Genesis 40 and 41). However, in the biblical narrative it is not man, but God, *non nobis Domine*, who provides the answer. One of the most colorful dreams is recorded on a stela of Thutmosis IV: one day the young prince slept in the shade of the sphinx, which was half-buried in the sand. The god Harmakhis appeared to him in a dream complaining about the neglected condition of the statue. When he became pharaoh, Thutmosis remembered the dream and uncovered the sphinx to its base.

Spending a night in a temple to receive a premonitory dream was a common practice. Sacred scribes, or *lector priests*, enjoyed a great reputation for interpreting dreams. The dream-oracle was an important method by which the gods revealed themselves.

Repeatedly I observed in the 1950s and 1960s young Copts in Upper Egyptian churches who had spent a night sleeping on a mat in front of the altar-screen near the icon of the Holy Virgin or the local patron-saint. The purpose was to receive, either through a dream or vision, some assurance for certain personal future benefits, be it the choice of a right partner, the passing of examinations, or economic success. Although a fourth-century ecumenical synod in Laodicea, Phrygia had plainly and distinctly prohibited this practice, this custom was deeply embedded in the minds of many Christians in the Nile Valley, in spite of the outspoken contempt of the psalmist: "They are like a dream when one awakes, on awaking you despise their phantoms" (Psalms 73:20). Bishop Thomas of al-Qusiya said bishops have received instructions not to allow this practice in their dioceses and believes it is hardly practiced anymore.

It is no coincidence that the well-known dreams in the Joseph stories have appeared as a recurring theme in early Christian art. Joseph is not merely the dreamer, he is also the interpreter of dreams. In fact, he is the Old Testament prefiguration of the New Testament Joseph of Nazareth (Mt 2:13–23). Joseph's dreams are portrayed in several seventh-century Coptic textiles.

In Coptic theology, dreams are considered a legitimate method for ascertaining the truth. In nominations and elections of Coptic hierarchs dreams or visions by a devout Christian have often settled disputes of contending parties. Demetrius, the twelfth successor of St. Mark, was elected by his predecessor's vision. Benjamin I (623–662) dreamt of his own election to the patriarchate. For the identification of relics, Copts have often relied upon the dreams of pious persons. In fact, in several cases the identification of the remains of anonymous martyrs and the naming of relics were due to a dream or a vision by some priest, monk, or a devout layman. In the summer of 1994 some bodily remains were discovered under the floor of the narthex of the Church of St. Shenuda in Old Cairo. A dream by a monk of the Monastery of Abu Mina in Maryut identified the relics as those belonging to the fourth-century martyr Julius of Aqfahs (Tut 22 / October 2). There has been an unprecedented number of recent discoveries and acquisitions of anonymous relics, for example those of the Akhmim al-Hawawish, the Fayyum-Naqlun or the

Antinoë martyrs, whose identity has been solely established by dreams and visions.

In pre-Christian times every village had a shrine honoring a pagan deity. Since ancient times Christians and Muslims have continued to build altars for martyrs and tombs for sheikhs respectively alongside the banks of the Nile.

The 'Last Judgement'

Among the more conspicuous religious survivals is the common pharaonic representation of the 'Last Judgment' in the form of the 'weighing of the heart.' This theme as such is a universal *leitmotiv* expressing the human demand for ultimate justice in a world that suffers from lack of fairness and violations of personal rights. The weighing of the heart is the certain and just way to arrive at a moral/ethical judgement. Job bewailed his wretchedness and requested: "Let me be weighed in a just balance, and let God know my integrity" (Job 31:6). The Book of the Dead portrays the weighing of the heart of the deceased person. The divine judge, often Osiris, sometimes Re, is enthroned on a dais and watches the scene. Anubis placed the dead person's heart on one of the scales' pans, while Maat, a gracious little person wearing an ostrich-plume on her head, representing the weight of truth, is placed on the other. The ceremony is supervised by Thoth who records the result. Some forty-two assessors receive the confessions of the dead.

The Egyptian procedure for the 'weighing of the heart' was possibly the forerunner of the Byzantine portrayals of the 'Last Judgement,' the *Deutera Parousia*, or the tribunal of the soul. As divine Judge, Christ enthroned on a rainbow (Ezekiel 1:28) is flanked by the Virgin Mary and John the Baptist and attended by the Apostles and choirs of angels. In front of the throne of judgement (Psalms 9:8) with the Instruments of Christ's Passion, appear Adam and Eve as representatives of humanity. The archangel Michael, appearing in Roman military apparel, holds the scales in his left hand. With his sword in his right hand, he defeats Beelzebul, the prince of demons, who tries to pull down the beam of the balance. In one pan is the soul of the dead person, while on the other side demons add weights to pull down the balance. Interestingly, traditional Coptic iconography has abstained from portraying this theme. A monumental fresco of the Last Judgement (1573) covers the eastern wall of the refectory in the

Greek Orthodox Monastery of St. Catherine in Sinai. In the eighteenth and nineteenth centuries Coptic artists have portrayed the archangel Michael holding the scales in his left hand and a sword in his right hand to overcome Beelzebul the dragon.

Egyptian Funerary Customs

Some of the pharaonic funerary customs have survived in one form or another to the present day. Four different practices are selected to demonstrate their usage among modern Copts. They are: the significance of the *corpus incorruptum*; the usage of funerary paintings; the recognition of the death-bird; and the associations with the dead.

The Significance of the *Corpus Incorruptum*

From time immemorial the Egyptians had mummified their dead, a custom which was one of the 'mysteries' of the dwellers on the banks of the Nile. The discovery that the hot, dry desert sand arrested and prevented the decay of the exposed body led to the practice to support its 'incorruptibility' by using the various methods of mummification. The purpose of these procedures was to preserve bodily integrity after death, since survival after death was considered to be of utmost importance. Herodotus (II, 86–88) and Diodorus (I, 91) described in detail the various methods of mummification for the preservation of the body from decay so as to enable the spirit to reoccupy the physical frame.

Likewise for the Egyptian Christians, their faith in the biblical resurrection of the dead and in the life eternal demanded the certainty of the bodily integrity of the deceased. Did not the psalmist pronounce: "For Thou wilt not leave my soul in hell, neither wilt Thou suffer Thine Holy One to see corruption (Psalms 16:10)"? In his sermon on the "Resurrection of the Dead" (PL 39, 1599–1600) the Upper Egyptian archimandrite Shenute of Atripe (d. 451) reminded his monks that "even if your eyes be torn out, at your resurrection you'll appear with eyes. Should they decapitate you, you'll rise from the dead with your head. Should they cut off your limbs, you'll rise with all your members of the body. Even if they cut off your finger, your hand or your foot, you'll rise as a *soma pneumatikos*, as a spiritual body, with all parts of the body restored."[3] Quoting the Apostle Paul, Shenute emphasized that at the resurrection of the dead, the body, though sown in corruption, is raised in incorruption, sown in dishonor, it is raised in glory, sown a natural body, it is raised a spiritual body (1 Corinthians 15:42–44). According to Ancient Egyptian mythology, under the leadership of his brother Seth, Osiris was not merely killed, but his body was dismembered, later echoed by the remarks in Shenute's sermon. However, through the efforts of his family, Isis and Nephthys, his members were again joined together so as to enable him to experience the resurrection with the full integrity of the body. In addition, an unexpected youthfulness was bestowed upon his body. The Old Testament Job was assured: "Though after my skin worms destroy my body yet in my flesh I shall see God" (Job 19:26). The early church adopted in the Apostles Creed the formula of the 'resurrection of the flesh *(sarkos anastasis).*'

The Coptic reverence and veneration of the *corpus incorruptum* is repeatedly mentioned in the annals of the church. The Synaxar of Misra 29 (September 4) reports the deceitful theft of the relics of St. John Colobus, which in the latter part of the eighth century reposed in the Melkite Monastery of St. Antony near the Red Sea. Monks of the Monastery of St. Macarius disguised as Bedouins entered the Monastery of St. Antony and took as booty the *corpus incorruptum* of the fourth-century desert father. This is recorded in the sayings of Pope John IV (777–799) when he describes the relics being ceremoniously received in the Wadi al-Natrun and transferred to the Monastery of St. Colobus.

From the ninth to the twelfth centuries, ten Coptic popes, as well as the three Macarii (St. Macarius the Great, St. Macarius the Alexandrian, St. Macarius of Tkoou), and Martinius, an imperial minister (fifth century), were kept in long tubes enveloped in precious shrouds. By the seventeenth century, the papal necropolis was extended to include the relics of Pope John XI (1619–1629) and those of St. John Colobus. Alfred J. Butler, visiting the Monastery of St. Macarius in 1881, reported their being "in eight cases, each containing two bodies . . . loosely put together and so slender in make, that one may clearly see the shriveled forms of the patriarch lying like so many mummies in their coffins."[4] The belief in the incorruptibility of St. Macarius the Great is strengthened by an account in the *History of the Patriarchs of the Egyptian Church*. In the early years of his reign, the Tulunid governor *(mutawalli)* Khumarawaih ibn Ahmad ibn Tulun (881–896) visited the Monastery of St. Macarius where "he was shown the body of St. Macarius. He commanded that the body should be loosed from his shroud, and he took hold of his beard and it opened its eyes in Khumarawaih's face. Then the governor fell on his back and remained for an hour in a swoon without uttering a sound (HPEC II, ii, 113)."[5]

The patron saint of the Monastery of St. Bishoi is the fifth-century desert father Bishoi (Abib 8 / July 15). He fled from the Berber raid of 408 and found refuge near Antinoë. In the ninth century Ope Joseph (830–39) transferred the body of Bishoi to his monastery in the Wadi al-Natrun. That this 'incorruptible saint' remained the pride of the desert fathers is attested by the observation of the French naval officer C.S. Sonnini, who passed by the Monastery of St. Bishoi on January 14, 1778. There the monks importuned him to visit their monastery. They said they were in possession of the body of a saint, which was "as fresh and florid as if still alive (Travels, etc. 1799, 368)."[6] To this day, the monks of the Monastery of St. Bishoi insist on the incorruptibility of their patron, whose reliquary in the choir of the Church of St. Bishoi is ceremonially aromatized annually with a variety of traditional spices *(hanut)*.

It is remarkable how the Copts have maintained their concern for the incorruptibility of the body, which is a reflection of some of the literary contents of the *Egyptian Book of the Dead*. In his sermon on the resurrection of the dead, St. Augustine mentions the Egyptian Christians and their belief in the incorruptibility of the body and their faith in the resurrection (PL 39, vol. 39, pp. 1599–1600).[7]

The faith of many Copts is impressively reflected in the fourth-century Story of Joseph, the spouse of the Holy Virgin. Jesus mummifies the body of Joseph and says: "The stench of death shall not dominate you, your ears shall not rot, pus shall never exude from your body, your body shall remain firm for the day of the Heavenly Supper, O my beloved father."[8]

The renewed interest in the veneration of relics during the second half of the twentieth century has revived the admiration of the *corpus incorruptum* of the saints. Coffins with a glass lid were constructed to enable the faithful to venerate the body of the saint. Two illustrations of this practice demonstrate this 'survival.' In the Church of the Holy Virgin in Dimyat (Damietta) the incorruptible body of the nineteenth-century saint Sidhom Bishai (Baramhat 17, March 26, 1844) reposes in a coffin with a glass lid. In the Church of the Holy Apostles at the Red Sea Monastery of St. Antony reposes the incorruptible body of the eminent nineteenth-century theologian and bishop Yusab ibn al-Abahh of Girga (Coptic month Tuba 17, 1826). The monks of the Monastery of St. Antony have repeatedly insisted that the body of St. Yustus al-Antoni of Sarawa (1910–1976) also remained uncorrupted!

The Usage of Funerary Paintings

Another interesting 'survival' of pre-Christian funerary customs is the recent addition of saints' portraits on the silk coverings of the reliquary-tubes. Whereas in the past an icon attached above or near the reliquary identified the saint, this new practice may be seen as a revival of the famous pharaonic funerary masks or the encaustic Fayyum portraits. Whether this was consciously or unconsciously intended, we do not know. At any rate, the Fayyum portraits purposefully retained the appearance of the person in the *status perfectionis*. They were painted in their 'prime of life,' often in or around their thirtieth year. The new Coptic paintings of the church fathers on the reliquary-tube covers show the saint as an idealized person in advanced age with a long, white beard, a symbol of his spiritual transfiguration. This is the case with the portraits of St. Bishoi in his monastery, and those of Sts. Isidore and Moses the Black in the Monastery of al-Baramus. In the case of St. Abra'am of the Fayyum (d. Ba'una 3, June 10, 1914), of whom photos are still available, the portraits resemble the original photos. His body reposes in the museum east of the Church of St. Mercurius, Dair al-Azab, Medinet al-Fayyum.

The Recognition of the Death-bird

During my travels in Egypt in the 1950s and 1960s I have met in both Cairo and Upper Egypt with Coptic families in mourning. In the room of the deceased they had placed on the sill of the open window a dish with cereals. The purpose was to attract the death-bird that was to receive the soul of the departed and fly with it to the heavens. Without mentioning it to my Coptic friends, I was reminded of the ancient Egyptian ba, the itinerant soul of the deceased person. The *ba* is represented in the form of a bird with a human face. According to the funerary papyri, the *ba* preferred the open spaces, revisiting the places beloved by the deceased person. The *ba*, the spiritual principle, appears independently of its physical support, and acts on its own account as a kind of representative of its 'owner.'

For the Egyptian Christians in the sixth and seventh centuries the function of the death-bird carrying the soul of the departed to heaven was an integral part of their faith. This belief is shown on numerous Upper

Egyptian tombstones. There the death-bird appears together with various cross designs and the Greek letters *alpha* and *omega*. The bird is normally shown with extended wings, sometimes holding in its beak a cross or a flower. Around the neck the bird carries a *bulla*, a capsule often decorated with a small cross.

A variation of the belief in death-birds is mentioned by Edward W. Lane. Writing in 1835 he referred to the death-bird in connection with the souls of those killed in the war or by accident: "These green birds eat the fruits of Paradise and drink of its rivers."[9] Winifred S. Blackman writing a century later confirms this observation. She had been told that visitors to the cemetery who see a number of small green birds near the graves believe them to be the souls of the dead who lie buried there.[10]

Associations with the Dead

On the occasion of the great *mulid* of the Holy Virgin at the Upper Egyptian Monastery of the Virgin al-Muharraq at al-Qusiya, during the week of June 18–28 (Ba'una 14–21) I observed the widows and their daughters. The large cemetery is situated in the desert toward the west, outside the large monastery-compound.

The Copts referred to this visit to their relatives' tombs as *al-tala'*, meaning "going to the desert." The monks told me that the *fellahin* believe that the souls of the dead return to their graves, and that they expect their relatives to visit them. Moreover, it was widely believed that the dead still have the same needs as they had in life. This means that the body should be fed. This is reminiscent of pharaonic practice in which large jars of food were placed in the royal tombs.

In pre-Christian days, the "Opening of the Mouth" ritual used to restore to the deceased the full use of his mouth, enabling him to eat and to drink. This ritual reanimated the vital force of the person in the afterlife and thus enabled him to experience life in eternity in a manner resembling his earthly way of life. It is this deep-seated faith that has motivated the mourning women to serve their dead husbands' needs with eatables of every kind in the hope of satisfying their hunger.

Some of the women on their way to the cemetery had smeared blue dye on their hands and faces. As I looked at them, I was reminded of the remark by Herodotus: "Whenever a man dies, the females disfiguring their heads and faces with dirt . . . with the garments in disorder . . . and beating themselves severely."[11] On their heads the women carried large baskets with bread-rings *(kahk)*, sweet cakes, and all kinds of fruit, while others carried water in their *qullas* (earthenware vessels) to the grave. Eventually, these gifts would be distributed among the poor.

I saw some of the women crouching in front of the graves, others even scratching the mud-bricks of the tomb in order to get closer to their loved ones. Here and there, some women addressed their husbands or sons. For quite a while they seemed to converse with them. The belief that the dead not only listen but that they also speak is widely held by the people of the Middle East. It was reported that the Old Testament Prophet Samuel announced the destiny of the king after his death. He raised his voice and prophesied the end of the peoples' sacrilege and wickedness (Sirach 46:20). It was said that even the Prophet Elisha demonstrated the power of his prophecies from his tomb (Sirach 48:13).

In many parts of Upper Egypt I have seen desecrated and pillaged Coptic tombs, which reminded me of the age-old tradition of the professional Upper Egyptian royal tomb robbers. While the body of the deceased is properly shrouded and placed in his grave, often certain personal possessions—in the form of charms or a jar containing some money—are added. No doubt, these 'valuables' are the reason for the destruction and theft of a tomb.[12] These Coptic customs and practices merely illustrate the changelessness of the Egyptian way of life!

About the Egyptian Calendar

The Old Egyptian and Coptic calendar is perhaps the most obvious survival of all pharaonic usages and practices that have continued to live on in the customs of their Christian heirs. The thirteen months are named either according to a pharaonic deity or after one of the numerous religious festivals. The Egyptian year used to be divided into three seasons, each having four months, which reflected the agricultural life in the Delta and the Nile Valley. While twelve months consist of thirty days each, the thirteenth month has merely five, in leap years six. However, since the inauguration of the Aswan High Dam on January 15, 1971, the agricultural life cycle of the Egyptians has been dramatically and decisively changed. The silt that used to fertilize the fields and thereby provide natural nutrients is nowadays kept back by the High Dam. This means that the original seasons, as set forth by the calendar, have lost much of their significance for the *fellahin* and the agricultural industry. The Egyptian calendar months are:

1. *Tut* (September 11–October 10) is dedicated to Thoth, the lunar god in the form of an ibis. Owing to his many-sided talents, he was known as the scribe of the gods and of the divine word.
2. *Baba* (*Paopi*, October 11–November 9) commemorates the Opet cele brations honoring Amun's procession from Karnak to Luxor.
3. *Hatur* (November 10–December 9) is dedicated to the goddess Hathor, presented in the form of a cow (Dendera). She is the wife of Horus of Edfu.
4. *Kiyahk* (December 10–January 9) was the name of the vessel for weighing the incense for the funeral ceremonies. During this month the annual Osiris feasts were celebrated. Commemorating Osiris, Egyptians still plant lentils in moist cotton-wool and watch their growth.
5. *Tuba* (January 10–February 7) is the coldest season and reminds the Egyptian of the spelt swelling.
6. *Amshir* (February 8–March 9) is the season for the "feast of the fire."
7. *Baramhat* (*Phamenot*, March 10–April 8) commemorates the feast of Amenophis I, the first pharaoh of the Eighteenth Dynasty (1512–1505 BC). On *Baramhat* 7, Seth killed Osiris.
8. *Baramuda* (*Pharmouti*, April 9–May 8) reminds the Egyptians of the feast of Renenutet, the agricultural goddess in the form of a serpent
9. *Bashans* (May 9–June 7) received its name from the feast of the lunar god Chons, the son of Amun and Mut.
10. *Ba'una* (June 8–July 7) commemorates the famous Theban "Feast of the Valley," the journey of Amun to the temple of Hatshepsut and the tombs of the Theban necropolis.
11. *Abib* (July 8–August 6) was dedicated to the fertility goddess Ipet who appeared in the form of a hippopotamus.
12. *Misra* (August 7–September 4) commemorates the nativity of the sun god Re.
13. *Nasi* (September 5–September 10), the small month, is dedicated to Osiris.

While many Copts consider themselves to be the true sons and daughters of the pharaohs, the Coptic Orthodox Church regards the period from the fourth to seventh centuries as its 'golden era,' the age of the illustrious martyrs, hermits, and ascetes, theologians and doctors of the church, and the period in which their Christian faith defeated the idolatry and polytheism of the pagan world.

2

Egyptian Christians as Citizens of an Islamic Society in the Middle Ages

From the very beginning, the Church was faced with defining its attitude to the world in general and to the state in particular. The history of the Christian Church in both the Orient and the Occident supplies many illustrations of the various attitudes, which the Church has taken toward the state, ranging from ascetic withdrawal from the kingdoms of this world to almost complete identification with the purposes and goals of a government. The purpose of this chapter is to throw some light upon the attitude of the Orthodox Copts toward the state in general, and toward the Islamic state in particular.[13]

For the period under discussion there is a certain paucity of available literary documents which deal with the pertinent issues.[14] Our main source from the seventh to twelfth centuries is the *History of the Patriarchs*, which constitutes a collection of many historical incidents rather than a church history with its independent philosophy of history.[15] We have the writings of Abu al-Makarim,[16] and the fifteenth-century Islamic historian al-Maqrizi.[17]

Since the attitude of the Orthodox Copts toward the state depended heavily upon that of the state, more than of the respective governor, to the church, it seems advisable to commence our study with a brief review of the attitude of the Islamic state toward the *dhimmis*,[18] in this case the Orthodox Copts. This issue, however, has to remain marginal to our discussion, since it has been thoroughly investigated by scholars reporting on the political and social impact of Islam.[19]

It is our conviction that the various attitudes of the Coptic Church toward the state reflect, in some way or another, the highly ambiguous teachings of the Apostolic Church toward the state. Thus we discover that even within the canon of the New Testament there are three basic attitudes toward government: that of seeing in the state a divine institution (Romans 13:1–7); that of opposition to the state (Apocalypse 13); and that of acceptance of the state (St. Luke 7:1–10; St. Matthew 22:16–22). The theory of a possible fourth type, that of transformation, i.e., the transformation of a pagan state into a so-called Christian state, which finds its first theological justification in the writings of the Christian apologists, obviously plays no role in our discussion.

The Attitude of the State Toward the Copts

In order to understand the attitude of Orthodox Copts toward the Islamic state it is necessary for us to recall the state's attitude toward the dhimmis, especially with regard to the Copts. The relationship of their church to the state was always heavily dependent upon the attitude the state adopted toward the Christians. Theoretically, there are three possible policies and attitudes the state could take toward religion: persecution, sufferance, and freedom. In persecuting the Copts an attempt would have been made to compel all Copts to submit to Islam. The consequence of this policy would have led either to the forceful conversion of all Copts to Islam, or to the general annihilation of those who refused to accept the new faith. In this connection it should be noted that the Coptic Synaxarium[20] lists only fifty "new martyrs," i.e., those Christians who suffered martyrdom during the Islamic period.[21] Sufferance, on the other hand, constitutes a compromise dependent upon the payment of a price, either in the form of taxes or in the surrender of certain privileges. Religious freedom and religious equality are relatively recent principles that are based upon the doctrine of the separation of church and state, a concept which is utterly alien both to Islam and Oriental Christianity.

According to Islamic jurisprudence, the *dhimmis* represent the tolerated non-Muslim communities within Islam. They included not only the so-called *ahl al-kitab*, or 'People of the Book,' but also certain idolaters and fire-worshipers. The *ahl al-kitab* or Scriptuaries were the Jews, Christians, Samaritans, and Sabians, that is, all those non-Muslims who possessed a Scripture. "Lo! Those who believe (in that which is revealed unto thee, Muhammad), and those who are Jews, and Christians, and Sabaeans—whoever believeth in Allah and the Last Day and doeth right—surely their reward is with their Lord, and there shall no fear come upon them neither shall they grieve."[22]

The *dhimmis*, who in Egypt were represented primarily by the Orthodox Copts, had to pay the poll tax, and in return they were officially entitled to full protection against any possible encroachment and molestation. It has also been maintained that the poll tax was in lieu of military service, though this view can hardly be upheld if one realizes that the Arabs looked upon military service as a privilege rather than as a burden. Sufferance, therefore, was one of the distinguishing marks of the policy of the invading Arabs, though in actuality, the degree of toleration depended largely upon the whims of the vizier or wali. The poll tax was collected from all Orthodox Copts except women, children, the poor, the blind, the sick, the insane, the unemployed, and—at least in the beginning—the monks. Yet, at the time of the patriarchate of Alexander II (705–730) 'Umar, the son of 'Abd al-Aziz, commanded that the poll tax should be collected from all men who would not become Muslims, even in cases where it was not customary to take it. The *dhimmis* in early Muslim Egypt were the victims of "frequent and seemingly haphazard changes in the status and in the levels and incidence of taxation."[23] In addition to the poll tax, those Copts who were landowners were also under obligation to pay the *kharaj*, or land-tax.

The major difficulty for the Orthodox Copts under Muslim rule, however, was their responsibility and their obedience to two social orders, the church and the state, and the superstructure within which the church existed. Since the demands of the church and the state were frequently at variance, in spite of the official Islamic attitude of sufferance, the Copts often found themselves in situations that demanded a choice of loyalty between the church and the state. Thus, for failure to obey the state, the Copts experienced persecutions, either in form of increased taxes or in actual prohibitions of the execution of their religious life. Otherwise, except for those instances mentioned in the *History of the Patriarchs of the Egyptian Church* and by al-Maqrizi, the Copts rarely found themselves in a position of having to apostatize to save their lives. True, the Copts experienced various degrees of pressure by the Muslim authorities to submit to Islam and many Copts succumbed to the frequent intimidations. Moreover, to abandon Christianity for Islam brought privileges, and in many instances pardon for past offences, whereas to abandon Islam and join the Christian Church was interpreted as treason and punishable as such. For example, we hear that during the patriarchate of Michael I (744–768) twenty-four thousand Copts in and around Cairo accepted Islam, which exempted them from paying the poll tax and relieved their economic burden. In addition to being exempt from the payment of the poll tax, some converts were granted special favors. For example, Peter, the deacon, who had approached the Caliph to write to the governor of Egypt for an appointment as patriarch, eventually became a Muslim, and was known as Abu al-Khair. He was presented with many gifts, garments, money, horses, and female slaves. During the reign of al-Mutawakkil (847–861) many Christians denied the Lord Jesus Christ. Some denied Him on account of the worldly possessions which they loved, and others on account of the poverty which they suffered.

Theoretically, Muslim law provided for the maintenance of the status quo of the Copts and guaranteed the security of Christian properties, provided, of course, that no new churches were added to those in existence. The Coptic Church was given some safety at the price of abstaining from proselytizing Muslims; what proved to be more disastrous, however, was the emergence of a situation in which the heads of the church were subjected to a constant temptation to unworthy subservience and intrigue. Indeed, the attitude of sufferance by the state was conditional upon the acceptance of an inferior social and political status.

Yet, in spite of the inferior status that Copts had to accept, the government continued to employ them in the civil service, especially as secretaries and clerks. For that matter, all provincial officials during the first hundred years of the Arab occupation, until the end of the Ummayad period, were Copts, and Coptic officials continued to collect the annona corn which was sent to Medina. The fact that many Christians were retained by the Muslim authorities as government employees, however, did not mean power or prestige, for Christians were not placed in positions where they could execute any authority over Muslims. And wherever Christians served as viziers, they held no absolute power. A Coptic tradition pertaining to the role of the Coptic clerk in the government is related by Abu al-Makarim (thirteenth century): "The Copts shall be of service to the faithful (Muslims) in their piety by taking care of their worldly problems."[24]

It is impossible, of course, to generalize, since the attitude of the various Muslim rulers toward the Christians showed marked differences. The

Fatimids (969–1171) were generally friendly toward them. Outstanding was al-'Aziz (975–996) who married a Christian wife and appointed her two brothers as patriarchs of Jerusalem and Alexandria, respectively. His son, al-Hakim (996–1021), however, was an exception who persecuted Christians and destroyed churches. The Ayyubids (1171–1250), on the other hand, dismissed many Christian secretaries from the diwan of Sultan Salah al-Din (1171–1193). He prohibited Christians from becoming government clerks and physicians. Yet, in spite of these dismissals, many Copts were soon reinstated, for their services appeared to be indispensable in the management of business.

The Coptic Interpretation of History

Following the Judaeo-Christian tradition, the Copts adhered to the teleological view of history. This means that the Copts discern in the movements of history the guidance of a Divine Will, which directs the destinies of humanity in general, and their destinies in particular, in conformity with a cosmic plan and purpose. This providential or theocentric interpretation of history is clearly reflected in the annals of the church. The realization of this fact is essential to our understanding of the Coptic attitude to the world and the Orders of Creation. Thus, while believing, that God favors His People, i.e., the Copts, He will deal with the rest of mankind accordingly. It is believed that the prayer of St. Athanasius, twentieth Patriarch of Alexandria (326–373), caused the destruction of princes who had maintained a heterodox theology. Moreover, the heretics were fought by the prayers of the orthodox, the supplication of the Copts finally led to the installation of a believing sovereign, namely Theodosius (379–395). God's partiality extended to the point that during the patriarchate of John III (677–686) God was held responsible for the punishment of the governor's wife with a sickness because of the wickedness of her husband, who had imprisoned the patriarch. Here, God employed the widespread oriental practice of vendetta, taking revenge on the wife of the culprit.

Interestingly enough, however, the Copts did not merely interpret their own relations with the rest of mankind through the eyes of Divine Intelligence. All historical events, whether they pertained to their affairs or not, were brought into the realm of the Divine Will. When 'Abdallah's forces totally annihilated Marwan II's (744–750) troops with God's help, it was God who gave 'Abdallah the victory over Marwan. This victory was achieved because of Coptic interference in the history of Islam. Indeed, the Copts believed that the fall of the despised Ummayad Dynasty was effected by the prayers of the monks in the Monastery of St. Macarius, who "assembled all the holy fathers and monks, and began to pray in the church night and day, crying to the Lord Christ to look upon us, and to take away our misery and all that men were suffering by captivity and slaughter and pillage. So the gracious God heard them, and raised up the Abbasids to help them, and they did not cease slaughtering them until they reached the Wadi Habib in answer to the prayers of the saints."

A theocentric interpretation was also engaged to provide meaning for the frequent persecutions. Suffering and martyrdom were always explained either from a soteriological point of view or given eschatological significance. The author of the Proverbs had warned and exhorted: "My son, despise not thou the chastening of the Lord, nor faint when thou art rebuked of him: For whom the Lord loveth he chasteneth, and scourgeth every son whom he receiveth. If you endure chastening, God dealeth with you as with sons"[25] (Proverbs 3:11). Aware of this warning, the Copts interpreted their suffering from the persecutions as ordained by God, and Shenute I, fifty-fifth Patriarch of Alexandria (859–880), could lament: "Of what is the Church of God guilty, that He shall bring down upon it this great trial?" the answer is given by the patriarch himself when he considers the persecutions as the legitimate punishment of God "on account of my sins." Yet, according to the Divine Plan, the chastening is a temporary and merely a cleansing act of God, for ultimately, "God preserveth His elect and leaveth them not to see corruption. Those whom He employs in the chastening of His People, He will punish with diseases and other calamities."

The Arab conquest and the subsequent Muslim administration was interpreted as a "chastening which descended from heaven from the Lord Christ upon all the Christians, and it overtook even others besides them of the nations, in order to punish them for all their offences in this world, and to save them in the next life." As David had said: "Blessed is the man whom the Lord shall chasten" (Psalm 94:12–13). Or as Solomon had said: "O my son, be not discontent at the chastening of the Lord, for who the Lord loveth, He chasteneth" (Proverbs 3:11a, 12a).

For the Copts, the destiny of their church rests in the hands of God. Success and failure, tranquility and persecutions, the building as well as the destruction of their churches and monasteries, indeed, everything was ascribed to the omnipotent will of God, who deals with His people according to their righteousness and holiness. As we have seen, persecutions as well as particular destructions of churches and monasteries were regarded as expressions of the Divine Purpose. When the famous Church of St. Michael on the Island of Cairo was destroyed, it was obvious, that this destruction was due to the multitude of sins committed by Macarius II, sixty-ninth Patriarch of Alexandria (1102–1128).

Good and evil, joy and suffering are all within the will of God, though for His elect, in spite of their tribulations, there is always hope, for His people there is the eternal promise of the ultimate and final victory.

The Attitude of the Orthodox Copts Toward the State

A Comparison: The Situation in the West

The ambiguity of the attitude of the Apostolic Church toward the state was somehow solved in the Latin West and in the Byzantine East. In the West, Pope Gelasius (492–496) had laid down the doctrine that both emperor and pope were supreme, each in his own sphere, and that the church was to live alongside the state. The church was to be regarded autonomous in spiritual matters, and its principal responsibilities were the custody of the Divine Sacraments and the concern for the Life Eternal. Yet, ever since the days of the Imperial Edict of Toleration in the fourth century, emperors had increasingly taken upon themselves certain ecclesiastical responsibilities. Constantine the Great (324–337) called himself an 'external bishop,' and Constantius (337–361) not only intervened at ecclesiastical councils, but considered his will as canonically binding. Both Constantine and Constantius, however, were superseded by Justinian (485–565), who pushed his spiritual caesarism like no other sovereign. His aim was complete religious uniformity and the inclusion of all subjects within one church dominated by himself. This naturally implied the vigorous suppression of all heretics, especially the Copts. The last powerful caesaro-papist in the West was Charlemagne (743–814), who exercised an unlimited power and authority over the papal states. When Pope Leo III (795–816) was driven out of the City of Rome by a violent insurrection, he took refuge with Charlemagne and appealed for reinstatement. Charlemagne proceeded to Rome where he held a great council of clergy and laity. The emperor nominated bishops, prescribed fasts, and convened synods. With the emergence of clericalism in the West, however, caesaro-papism steadily declined. On the other hand, in the Byzantine East, caesaro-papism remained the official policy of the state toward the church for many centuries to come.

While caesaro-papism stood for the supremacy of the secular and political authority over the church, clericalism advanced the interests of the church in purely secular and political realms. Yet, it was not until 1122, the Concordate of Worms, that the emperor surrendered his spiritual authority. Like caesaro-papism, clericalism found its justification in the Canon of Holy Scriptures. "And they said, Lord, behold, here are two swords. And he said unto them, it is enough" (Luke 22:38). By the eleventh century, the two swords had come to symbolize the two great powers in this world, and the problem of their relations with each other had given rise to innumerable controversies. On one point, however, all the disputes were agreed. Both swords were within the church. The unity of a Christian civilization was perfected during the Middle Ages, and the establishment of papal supremacy over the secular powers was an accomplished fact. Indeed, the popes were not merely heads of the church, but heads of 'Christendom,' the heads of a culture.

For the Oriental churches, however, which from the middle of the seventh century onwards lived under Muslim rule, neither a Christian caesaro-papism nor a hierachical clericalism provided possible solutions for the problems regarding their attitudes and policies toward the state. Indeed, the Oriental Churches in general, and the Coptic Church in particular, never demonstrated a coherent and consistent attitude toward the state. Thus we find that even within relatively brief periods, the attitudes of the Copts toward the state changed from one extreme to another. In the Coptic Church, the apostolic ambiguity regarding church-state relations appears to have been carried through the centuries, often in a highly opportunistic manner.

Because of the lack of a definite policy, it might appear utterly presumptuous to establish certain types of attitudes toward the state. Nevertheless, one can detect at least three distinct attitudes that can be deduced from the records. Save for a few exceptions, I have limited the investigation to the principal document, the *History of the Patriarchs of the Egyptian Church*, and from an analytical study of this source, the following attitudes of the Coptic Church toward the state emerge:

1. Identification of the state as a divine institution;
2. Opposition to the state;
3. Mutual acceptance between church and state.

The Church's Identification of the State as a Divine Institution

Theoretically, the Pauline doctrine of the divine origin of the state dominated the attitude of the Copts toward government. The positive attitude of the Egyptian Christians toward government may have been influenced by the ancestral belief in the divine origin of government, which had been taught in the Nile Valley from days immemorial. Pharaohs, kings, and caliphs have profited ever since from the almost instinctive subservience of the Egyptians to governmental authority. Therefore, the Pauline doctrine, as stated in Romans 13:1–7, was readily received by the Egyptians, who were well prepared for its acceptance on account of their pre-Christian attitude toward the state. The ancient Egyptians believed the pharaohs to be divine by birth, and the pharaoh's decrees were considered as being of divine authority.

Numerous instances in the history of the church lead one to believe that the Copts, to whom the church is the visible manifestation of God's will, saw in the Muslim government an institution of divine origin. When the Bashmurites (a certain Christian sect) gathered to revolt against the government, Joseph, the fifty-second Patriarch of Alexandria (830–849), admonished them severely, citing in his support the words of the Apostle: "Whosoever therefore resisteth the power, resisteth the ordinance of God; and they that resist shall receive to themselves damnation" (Romans 13:2). This fundamentally positive attitude toward the state enabled the Copts to interpret certain actions, deliberations, and sayings of the Muslims as 'acts of God.' Moreover, the Copts apparently saw no difficulties in ascribing to a Muslim the ability to speak the 'Word of God,' and God could employ Muslim governors for the execution of His will. Hisham (724–743) is called by the Copts "a God-fearing prince." The Christians prayed for him and God gave him a prosperous reign; he ruled for twenty-two years. The chronicler of the *History of the Patriarchs of the Egyptian Church* records that "the amir al-Guyus, the governor, spoke to the patriarch and the bishops through the inspiration of God the Exalted because he was a king, even as Solomon the Wise said: 'The heart of the king is in the hand of God.' Then he demanded that the Christians should pray for him." The governor also "through the inspiration of God" commanded the Copts to draw up for him a collection of "Canons of Religion" and to present these canons to him. The canons became the thirty-four canons of Cyril II, the sixty-seventh Patriarch of Alexandria (1078–1092). Evidently, these new canons, which prohibited the widely practiced sale of ecclesiastical offices (simony), and stipulated that in case of disputes, priests and laity should not resort to the government authorities, but rather turn to their bishop, were frequently broken. Consequently, the governor ordered the patriarch and the bishops to attend a council, and in a manner reminiscent of the great Western caesaro-papists, the governor reminded the patriarch of the canons of the Christian faith and reiterated the observance of the new canons, which were written upon order of the government. During the governorship of al-Guyus, the involvement of the state in purely ecclesiastical affairs increased to the point that it was even the governor rather than the patriarch who assigned churches to the Syrians and to the Armenians in the Monastery of al-Khandaq (outside of Cairo).

From the time of the Arab conquest onwards, the Muslim governors recognized the patriarch as holding an official public office. Therefore, nominees to the supreme ecclesiastical office had to be presented to the respective governor for confirmation. In the latter part of the seventh century, the bishops and the laymen had nominated a certain George to be patriarch without consulting Amr 'Abd al-'Aziz, the governor. When the he heard of it, he cancelled George's nomination and commanded them to appoint Isaac, who became the forty-first Patriarch of Alexandria (686–689). Sometimes, the Copts not only followed the governor's order, but even considered his choice as being from God. All patriarchal candidates had to be examined by the governor prior to their enthronement, though, again, there are some instances when the Copts questioned the governmental authority for the confirmation of their candidate. When Isaac's successor, Simon I, the forty-second Patriarch of Alexandria (689–701) was nominated, he was presented to the governor. At the same time, however, the Copts pointed out that the choice was a matter which belonged to God, and that of the governor was secondary. These two instances, which dealt with the same issue, illustrate well the inconsistency of the Coptic attitude toward the state.

In spite of the fact that the patriarchs were frequently pressed to demonstrate their loyalty to the state, the patriarchs nevertheless abstained from swearing oaths at all. The opposition to the practice of swearing an oath they justified by quoting the biblical admonition: "But above all things, my brethren, swear not, neither by heaven, neither by the earth, neither by any other oath: but let your yea be yea; and your nay, nay; lest ye fall into condemnation" (St. James 5:12; St. Matthew 5:34–36).

On the other hand, there are instances when the Copts approached the governor with the request to interfere in the appointment of a patriarch. In the latter part of the eighth century, "the Coptic bishops and notables called on the governor to write to the seniors of Wadi Habib, that they might give up Abba Michael (744–767) to the bishops so as to make him a patriarch."[27] A similar affair occurred following the death of John VI, the seventy-fourth Patriarch of Alexandria (1189–1216), when the See of Alexandria remained vacant for eighteen years. On the occasion of Sultan al-Malik al-Kamil's visit (1218–1238) to the Monastery of St. Macarius in the Wadi al-Natrun, the monks complained to him of their lack of a patriarch.

There are some cases reported where the governor refused the appointment of a patriarch on the grounds that the necessary fees had not been paid. The authorization in certain periods depended upon the payment. In the case of Joseph (830–849), the governor did not authorize the appointment by saying: "Isaac has sent to me and promised me 1,000 dinars, if he shall sit upon this throne." Yet, the Copts remained firm in their nomination, and finally Joseph was made patriarch. Whenever disputes regarding the selection and nomination of a successor to the patriarchal throne arose, Copts readily went to the government authorities. Thus, following the death of Shenute II, the sixty-fifth Patriarch of Alexandria (1032–1046), there arose disagreement pertaining to the nomination of a successor, and one party, consisting of the priests of Alexandria, approached the sultan and his vizier to accuse the other party of nominating an unsuitable candidate. Indeed, one of the functions of government in terms of its relationship with the church was that of serving as mediator between alienated parties within the Coptic Church. Shaikh Abu Zikri Yahya ibn Macarius, the chief of the diwan of the state, mediated between Christodoulos, the sixty-sixth Patriarch of Alexandria (1047–1077), and a party of dissatisfied bishops, who demanded the deposition of the patriarch.

The tragic disunity among Christians was another factor which caused the involvement of the state in the exclusive affairs of the church and thereby strengthened the position of the state. The various parties within the church used to approach the government accusing each other in front of the Sultan, but just as often, the government would enter the disputes for the sake of maintaining peace within the church. The governor, being theologically and ecclesiastically detached from the issue, often served as mediator and arbitrator.

During the first few centuries of Muslim rule, both Greek Orthodox and Copts called upon the government authorities and brought their claims and rights to their attention. Theodore, the Patriarch of the Chalcedonians, approached Yazid I, the son of Mu'awiyah (680–683), the Caliph in Damascus, and received a diploma from him giving him authority over the people of Alexandria, Maryut, and all neighboring districts, which caused severe sufferings to the Copts. The question of the property of the Church of St. Menas was taken to 'Abd al-Malik, the governor of Egypt, and both the Copts and the Greek Orthodox disputed matters concerning the true orthodoxy of their confessions, as well as the respective historical claims of the church, before the governor. Finally, so the Coptic chronicler joyfully reports, the judge decided upon the property right of the Church of St. Menas in favor for the Copts.

Personal matters, like rivalries and ambitions, which were presented by members of the Coptic clergy to the governor caused hardship and privations for many Christians. For example, Benjamin, a deacon, leveled accusations against his fellow Christians to the governor, an act which led to the introduction of a poll tax for monks, and Peter the deacon went to the caliph with bribes and asked him to instruct the governor of Egypt to appoint him patriarch. A great deal of suffering and several imprisonments of the patriarch (Shenute I, 859–880) were the result of the accusations by his own people. First a monk of the Ennaton Monastery, and later a deacon of al-Basmur brought accusations against the patriarch before the governor, which in each case led to his imprisonment. Sometime later, a monk informed the government that the patriarch had engaged in proselytizing Muslims, a false accusation which caused considerable hardship.

One of the severest persecutions against the Copts happened under al-Hakim bi-'Amr Allah and was was instigated by a monk. John of the Monastery of St. Macarius, who had witnessed a number of people purchasing the episcopate for money, requested to be appointed bishop without payment. However, his wish was not granted, so he began writing letters against the patriarch to al-Hakim. Thereupon, the patriarch was imprisoned and cast to the lions; many churches were destroyed in consequence.

State involvement in purely ecclesiastical affairs increased throughout the centuries, largely on account of financial revenues, which the government extracted whenever an opportunity availed itself. Soon after the Arab conquest, episcopal consecrations required the authorization of the governor. "A priest from the people of the Indies came to Abba Simon (689–701) to ask him that he would ordain for him a bishop for the Indies. The patriarch replied: 'I cannot ordain a bishop for you without the command of the amir.'" Therefore, instead of approaching the ecclesiastical authorities, ambitious priests bribed the governor into ordering the patriarch, Abba James (819–830), to make them bishops. The Nubian and the Ethiopian kings had to request bishops for their vacant dioceses from the governor in Cairo rather than from the patriarch, and complaints about the Egyptian dignitaries were addressed to the state rather than the spiritual authorities. Indeed, under constant state financial pressure the clergy became so morally corrupt that by the eleventh century the chronicler lamented: "The Lord did not endure the deeds of his bishops, for they were become as walis who lorded over the priests. They invented pretexts for collecting money by every means and they trafficked in the Church of God on account of the love of silver and gold. Moreover, it had to be decided that a deacon or any other person who had decried a priest and departed from the judgment of the church and had sought aid from the Sultan or the Qadi be either suspended from his office or be forbidden to receive the Divine Mysteries."

The foregoing description clearly illustrates the dependence of the Coptic Church to the state. However, it is important for us to remember that at certain times the Copts may have been so intimidated by the authorities, that for the sake of preservation, they were willing to attribute any kind of authority to a government which, in actuality, they despised.

The Church's Opposition to the State

The Egyptian Christians did not follow the dictates of the government blindly. Whenever the government openly persecuted the church, the Copts adopted the classical attitude of passive resistance as prescribed by the visionary of the Apocalypse. "Here is the patience and the faith of the saints" (Revelation 13:10b). There are numerous instances recorded when the Copts regarded the government as being inherently evil, and to be condemned for its wickedness. There were some Copts who interpreted the Arab conquest as a deliverance from Byzantine oppression. Others soon realized that their new masters were not much different in their attitude to them, and John, Bishop of Nikiou, describing the Arab conquest, said: "The yoke they laid on the Egyptians was heavier than the yoke which had been paid on Israel by Pharaoh. Him God judged by a righteous judgment by drowning him in the Red Sea after He had sent many plagues both on men and cattle. When God's judgment lights upon these Muslims, may He do unto them as He did aforetime unto Pharaoh."[28] Christians called 'Umar ibn 'Abd al-'Aziz (717–720) the Antichrist, who was ultimately to be destroyed by God, because he enforced the payment of the poll tax on those who were previously exempted. The Copts believed that God deposed al-Qasim (eighth century) due to his evil deeds. Yet, at the same time, except for the unsuccessful Coptic revolts between 726 and 773, Coptic opposition to the state confined itself to theological denunciations. A systematic and consistent attitude of opposition to the government, however, never emerged among the Copts, despite many oppressive and discrimatory edicts by governors and caliphs. Thus, the negative attitudes of the Copts toward the state were caused largely by temporary and symptomatic situations.

In this connection, it is interesting to note that the Copts produced few apologetic works with regard to the teachings of Islam as a Christian heresy, like John of Damascus who relates how in the days of Emperor Heraclius a false prophet arose among the Arabs. On the contrary, it can be said that, though the Copts had to respect the government, they abhorred the teachings of Islam.[29]

In times of persecution, Christians made representations to the government. Thus, for example, several Christian notables complained to al-Mu'tazz (866–868) about their oppression and the destruction of churches. The clergy, on the other hand, frequently adopted a more passive attitude, "and because of the intensity of their fear, the bishops and the priests used to put on the dress of laymen and alter their clothes," while the patriarch occasionally would go in hiding.[30]

Mutual Acceptance between Church and State

As pointed out, from the very beginning of the Arab conquest, the Islamic government in Egypt offered its protection to the Copts, thus creating an atmosphere of sufferance, which to the Copts was a welcome change from the oppressive policies of the Byzantine rulers. The general 'Amr ibn al-'As, the conqueror of Egypt, wrote a letter to Benjamin I, the thirty-eighth Patriarch of Alexandria (622–661), whose content gave the Copts great confidence in their religious future. "There is protection and security for the place where Benjamin is, and peace from God, therefore let him come forth secure and tranquil and administer the affairs of his church, and the government of his nation. . . . Resume the government of all thy churches and of all thy people. And if thou wilt pray from me, that I may go to the West and to Pentapolis, and take possession of them, as I have of Egypt, and return to thee in safety, I will do for these all that thou shalt ask of me."[31]

This attitude of mutual acceptance between the church and the state presupposed not only a certain degree of tolerance by the state, it also required a mutual recognition of the respective spheres of interest and responsibility. Often, however, these spheres of responsibility were not very clearly defined, and we discover the church engaging in social, economic, and legal matters, while the government was involved simultaneously either by request or by sheer necessity in affairs pertaining exclusively to the church.

Whereas the involvement of the Coptic Church in governmental affairs remained insignificant, that is in terms of general policy of the state, we do discover that the involvement of the state in ecclesiastical matters produced serious consequences. Whatever may have appeared as a legitimate concern and the application of the *ius circa sacra* (laws outside the jurisdiction of the church) soon developed into a situation in which the state felt itself justified to engage in the *ius in sacra* (religious laws/matters).

There are numerous instances when the government considered it to be advantageous to the solution of a particular problem to solicit the services of the church. For example, in the middle of the seventh century, Maslamah, a Muslim commander, appointed seven Coptic bishops to judge certain people in Sakha (a small town in the Nile Delta), who were accused of burning some clerks who happened to be employed there. About the same time, John III, fortieth Patriarch of Alexandria (677–686), engaged in government projects. He is reported to have initiated the construction of public works including a mill and a press for linseed oil, and he provided economic support for the poor and the needy by giving them food and money. Marwan I (683–685) even appointed two secretaries over the whole land of Egypt, Athanasius and Isaac, "who were both trustworthy and orthodox." Although mutual cooperation between church and state was practiced to a considerable extent, yet, at the same time, the church was expected to be subservient to the state, for whenever the governor visited Alexandria, the patriarch was expected to meet and to welcome him. Omittance of this gesture caused denunciation and rebuke by the Muslim authorities.

Simon I, forty-second Patriarch of Alexandria (689–701) is reported to have desired mutual acceptance and cooperation throughout his time in office, as the chronicler states: "he was striving to prevent difficulties between Christians and Muslims." Often, Copts went out of their way to demonstrate and publicize their good will so as to retain public respect. Mark II, forty-ninth Patriarch of Alexandria (799–819), saw himself able to pray for the governor: "May the Lord preserve thy days and exalt thee yet more and increase the power." At the same time, we ought to be cautious in our spiritual or political evaluation of the prayers offered by Christians for the government. It is impossible, of course, to prove their sincerity or insincerity. Yet, for the Copts the possibility always existed to pretend their allegiance to the state by offering prayers for the governor. Whenever possible, the Copts carried out government decisions, provided they did not harm their witness. For that matter, the patriarchs were charged with a threefold responsibility: they were to retain and encourage relations with their sister church, the Jacobite Patriarchate of Antioch; they were charged with the responsibility for their daughter-churches in Ethiopia and Nubia; and thirdly, they were to carry out the decrees issued by the governor of Egypt. In spite of persecution, the poll-tax payment, and discriminatory practices, many Christians maintained a positive attitude toward the state to the point of rendering public services to the government. Thus, we discover that Christians were repeatedly called upon to serve in important positions. In the middle of the ninth century, at a time when the Muslims were well established in Egypt, the superintendent of the treasury was a Christian, namely Abraham ibn Sawirus. We are told that the Caliph al-Mu'izz (969–975) even consulted Abraham, the sixty-second Patriarch of Alexandria (975–978) and "caused him [the patriarch] to be brought to him at all times to take his opinion on what concerned him and to receive his blessing."[32] The regard of al-Mu'izz for the church was so profound that he could say to the patriarch: "Desire of me something and I will do it for thee." Whereupon the patriarch said: "I desire nought, save that God may strengthen thy state, and give thee victory over thine enemies."[33] Finally, Abraham was permitted to restore the destroyed churches. Certainly, this was not an isolated incident. Christodoulos, the sixty-sixth Patriarch of Alexandria (1047–1078), was repeatedly honored by the amir al-Guyus at public occasions, and Cyril II, the sixty-seventh Patriarch of Alexandria (1078–1092), could pray for al-Mustansir (1035–1094) in his presence. Mutual respect, therefore, did exist occasionally, though, no doubt, this was as much a reflection of the respective personalities as it was the stated policy of the two institutions during those periods. For it should be remembered that the attitude of genuine and spontaneous acceptance and cooperation between the church and the state remained a rare phenomenon in the thirteen hundred years of Muslim rule in Egypt.

For the purposes of our typological analysis, we may be permitted to regard mutual acceptance as the third principal attitude which the Copts maintained with respect to their relation to the state. Theoretically, this attitude may reflect the biblical statement of the two realms as expressed by the words of Jesus: "Render unto Caesar the things that are Caesar's, and to God the things that are God's" (St. Mark 12:17). It goes without saying that this statement was almost impossible to implement, for once transformed into a policy, it clearly separates the church from the state. Though desirable, yet this policy can be executed only by a sympathetic, and religiously neutral state. And while outwardly at least there existed a separation of church and state at the time immediately following the Arab conquest, it has been shown that it proved to be impossible to maintain this separation. True, John III, the fortieth Patriarch of Alexandria (677–686), could still say to 'Abd al-'Aziz, the governor: "The governor's command is obeyed in what is right, but his orders are disobeyed when they are displeasing to God, for our Lord said, 'Fear not those who kill the body and have no power over the soul, but rather fear him which is able to destroy both soul and body in hell.'" Or the statement by Joseph, the fifty-second Patriarch of Alexandria (830–849), "I do not resist the prince's command, but only unjust orders." These policy statements, which reflect the biblical teaching of the two realms, remained, however, largely theoretical. For a church that had always interpreted history from a theocentric point of view found it virtually impossible to carry through the distinction of the two realms. We have to remember, that sociologically speaking, the Coptic Church always retained its 'church characteristics,' and thus, fundamentally, an institutionalistic attitude toward the world in general and toward the state in particular. Sectarian isolation, therefore, was impossible for such an ecclesiastical institution, and mutual acceptance, whenever possible, seemed to be the logical consequence of the theory of the two realms.

On the other hand, those Copts who held radical sectarian attitudes with regard to the church-state relationship soon discovered that the only way to implement these attitudes consistently and coherently meant withdrawal either to the desert monastery or the desert cave.

3
The Christian Churches in Egypt

The Coptic Orthodox Church
Historical Note

According to the Gospel of St. Matthew, the Holy Family, fleeing from the wrath of Herod the Great, sought refuge in Egypt, where, according to local tradition, they stayed for a period of three years, until Herod's death in 4 BC. Many Copts believe that even prior to the beginning of the public ministry of Jesus Christ, Egyptians accepted the Divine Child as Lord over their lives. In fact, a wealth of stories and legends has been transmitted to us about the wonderous works performed by the Christ child in the Delta and the Nile Valley.

Foundation of the See of Alexandria

Following the visit to the Land of the Pharaohs by the Infant Christ, St. Luke informs us that Egyptians were present on the Day of Pentecost, when the Holy Spirit descended upon the faithful in Jerusalem. There is good reason to believe that at least some of these Egyptians returned to their homes, where they established Christian congregations. The Christians of Egypt are convinced that St. Mark the Evangelist visited Alexandria, where he preached the Gospel and founded the See of Alexandria. Moreover, it is generally believed that St. Mark received the crown of martyrdom in Alexandria. The apostolic foundation of the Coptic Church is significant, as to this day the head of the Coptic church is called the Pope of Alexandria. The current pope, Shenuda III, is the 117th Patriarch of the See of St. Mark.

The history of the Coptic Church is both glorious and tragic. Glorious in the number of her illustrious sons, such as Sts. Athanasius, Cyril, Antony, and Pachomius, to mention but a few; and tragic in the vast number of her children, who in the various persecutions suffered martyrdom for their adherence to the Christian faith. These are commemorated to this day by the Coptic Calendar in which the years are dated from the Year of the Martyrs (am, Anno Martyrum), which recalls the great persecution of the Christians that began in Egypt in 303 during the reign of Emperor Diocletian (284–311). For this reason Christians have made the Era of the Martyrs commence on August 29, 284, the year in which Diocletian became emperor. Following Diocletian's persecutions in Egypt from 303–311, Egyptian Christianity emerged victorious and dynamic, so much so that its theology and Christology were to leave a lasting impression upon the whole church. Though there is no question that the Greek element in Egypt played an important role in this development, men like St. Antony and St. Pachomius were Egyptians who were hardly touched by the Greek atmosphere which permeated Alexandria.

The Didascalia

The outstanding contribution of Alexandrian Christianity to the Universal Church was the Didascalia, the famous Catechetical School, where Christian scholars labored to prove that reason and revelation, philosophy, and theology were not only compatible but also essential for each other's comprehension. The first great scholar to serve as head of the Didascalia was Pantaenus. Although his exegetical contributions are lost, we can reconstruct some of his theological tenets by employing the testimony of his contemporaries. For this information, we are dependent on Clement, his successor, and on Origen. Authorities say that Pantaenus most probably came to Alexandria about the year 180, when he was appointed head of the School of Catechumens and remained there until he died shortly before 200. He was followed by Clement of Alexandria, the most illustrious pupil of Pantaenus, who was probably born of pagan parents about 150, and who died in Jerusalem around 220. Upon the death of Pantaenus, Clement became the head of the Catechetical School. When the severe persecutions of Septimius Severus compelled him to leave Egypt, he sought refuge in Cappadocia.

The most important theologian and most prolific author was Origen, whose life can be divided into five sections: his youth; his scientific and religious activities; his travels; his stay at Caesarea in Palestine; and his sufferings and death. Born of Christian parents in 185, Origen joined the

Catechetical School at an early age where he listened to the lectures of Pantaenus and Clement. Intensely ascetic by nature, he observed the most rigorous vigils and earned just enough from copying manuscripts to provide for his physical needs. A rash decision led him to apply the literal interpretation of St. Matthew 19:12 by castrating himself. Origen worked in Alexandria for twenty-eight years, from 204–232. It was during this period that he traveled to Rome, Arabia, Antioch, and Palestine. In Palestine the bishops invited him to deliver public lectures in the churches. Moreover, it was here that he was ordained presbyter, an act which Demetrius of Alexandria interpreted as an infringement of his own right. Demetrius convened two synods: the first gathering resolved to banish Origen from Alexandria; the second determined that he was to be defrocked. In 232, having settled in Caesarea, Origen established a flourishing school, and some of his pupils, for example Gregory Thaumaturgos, Bishop of Neocaesarea, rose to important positions in the hierarchy. Origen continued to travel to Cappadocia, Nicomedia, Athens, and Arabia. During the Decian persecution he suffered maltreatment, and though he survived these troubles, he died at Tyre in 253. Among his exegetical and theological writings, there is the *Hexapla*, in which he placed the Hebrew text side by side with the various Greek versions. Then there are the exegetical works, which are divided into the *scholla*, the homilies, and the commentaries. The principal apologetic work is his book *Against Celsus*, a second-century pagan philosopher. This work, written in Caesarea, has been preserved completely.

Origen was succeeded as head of the Catechetical School of Alexandria by Heracles, his former pupil and assistant. Little is known about him. After the death of Demetrus, Heracles succeeded him on the throne of St. Mark in Alexandria. The successor of Heracles as head of the Didascalia was another famous pupil of Origen, Dionysius of Alexandria, later surnamed 'the Great.' In AD 231 he was head of the Catechetical School, and in AD 248 he became bishop of Alexandria. During the Decian persecution he fled to the Libyan desert, and under Valerian he was banished to Cephro. Faced with the problem of the apostates, Dionysius readmitted them and prohibited the rebaptism of penitent heretics.

In one of his letters, Dionysius (d. 264) referred to his predecessor Heracles, who had defended orthodox teaching, as "our blessed pope Heracles." It should be noted that this is the first time that the head of the church of Alexandria is accorded the title pope *(papas)*, which was some fifty years before that same title was applied to the bishop of Rome.[34] Dionysius' successors, Maximus (264–282) and Theonas (282–300) had also served as heads of the Didascalia before their election to the throne of St. Mark.

The Canon of Holy Scripture

Egypt's role in the formation of the Canon of Holy Scriptures was of utmost importance, owing to the natural advantages of its position and the conspicuous eminence of its great teachers during the third century (Clement of Alexandria and Origen). The testimony of the Alexandrian Church to the New Testament Canon is generally uniform. In addition to the acknowledged books, the Epistles to the Hebrews and the Apocalypse were received there as Divine Scripture, even by those who doubted their immediate Apostolic origin. The two shorter Epistles of St. John were well known and commonly received, but no one, except Origen, so far as can be discovered, was acquainted with the Second Epistle of Peter.

Of Coptic versions, the Memphitic text did not include the *Apocalypse*, and it appears that it was not included in the Thebaic Canon of AD 356. Athanasius in one of his Festal Letters has given us a list of the books of the New Testament, the fountains of salvation, exactly agreeing with our Canon. In addition to these, he notices other books, and among them the *Teachings of the Apostles* and the *Pastor Hermes*, as useful for young converts, though they were not included in the Canon.

Theological Controversies

During the fourth and fifth centuries, theological and Christological controversies dominated the course of the history of the Egyptian Church. The significance of the Arian controversy with regard to its inner-Egyptian importance is seen by the roles of Meletius, the Arian Bishop of Lycopolis, and that of St. Athanasius, who emerged from the Arian controversy not merely as the orthodox patriarch of the Church of Alexandria, but also as the universally accepted and revered doctor of the Catholic Church. Alexandria's leading position within the church was further strengthened by its contribution of monasticism. Its dynamic impression upon the church ceases, however, during the second half of the fifth century. Whereas St. Antony and St. Pachomius were ascetes of universal significance, St. Shenute's impact was largely limited to Egypt, and specifically to Upper Egypt.

The Chalcedonian controversy, with Cyril I and Dioscorus I as the two principal personalities from the miaphysitic point of view, eventually led to the tragic schism which alienated the Church of Egypt from both the Byzantine and Latin churches. Egyptian national sentiment—a non-theological factor—may well have been an important issue in the unfortunate division of the Body of Christ. The post-Chalcedonian developments, i.e., the struggle for supremacy (dyophysite or miaphysite) in Alexandria, the irenic attempt of Zeno to settle with the *Henoticon* the theological estrangement by omitting the word 'nature' from the *Instrument of Union*, only led to additional schisms. At any rate, by the fifth century, the church was divided into Dyophysites, Miaphysites, Arians, and Nestorians.

By the beginning of the sixth century, several inner monophysitic divisions emerged, and thus weakened even further the witness of the Coptic, i.e., Egyptian Church. Moreover, the leadership within miaphysitism passed to the Syrian Church which for the following centuries determined the theological thinking of the miaphysites.

The Coptic Orthodox Episcopal Sees in Egypt

Abnub. Center of monasticism in the fifth to sixth centuries, with Dair Abu Buqtur al-Gabrawi, Dair al-'Adhra in Beni Riza, and Dair Abu Buqtur Shu where Pope Gabriel VIII (1585–1602) addressed Pope Sixtus V of Rome recognizing the supremacy of the Roman pontiff. The bishopric was established in June 1986 with the consecration of Bishop Luqa.

Abu Tig. An Episcopal See since the thirteenth century, with well-known medieval appointees, Bishop John (1257) and Murqus of Abu Tig (1320). Once part of the diocese of Naqada, Girga, and Asyut. In the eighteenth century Bishop Athanasius was one of ten Coptic bishops. Bishop Andarawus was consecrated for Abu Tig and Sidfa in June 1980. Sidfa, south of Abu Tig, was the birthplace of Pope John XIII (1484–1524), famous for the *mulid* of St. Bishoi on Abib 8 (July 8).

Akhmim *(Panopolis)*. Center of the fourth century persecutions. Martyrdoms of Apa Hamoi, Bishoi, Menas, Mercurius, Ephraim, Panine, Panei, Phoebammon and the eight thousand martyrs. Place of exile for Pope Athanasius, also for Sabellius and Nestorius of Constantinople. In 431 Bishop Sabinus went to Ephesus. In the Middle Ages, Akhmim was joined with Abu Tig (Yusab, 1250), sometimes with Ibsai (Cyril, 1598) and also with Girga (Yusab, 1769). It was also a center of monasticism: the Monastaries of Saint Bakhum, Sawama' Sharq, Apa Tuma, Malak Mikhail, Salamuni, Shuhada, al-'Adhra, Hawawish, Sabat Gebel, Bir al-'Ain, Mari Girgis Iqa'iwa Sharq, Apa Bisada, Minsha. Bishop Bisada was consecrated for Akhmim and Saqulta in June 1980.

Al-Arish *(Rhinocoloura)*. Aktisanes of Ethiopia, contemporary with Amosis II (Twenty-sixth Dynasty), used to sever the noses of criminals and settled them in the town, according to Seneca, Strabo, and Stephen of Byzantium. Bishops Salomon, Melas, Solon, Polybius, Hermogenes and Zeno (fifth century) are known from the Chronicles. Here Noah distributed his inheritance to Shem, Ham, and Japhet (*Epiphanius, Adv. Haer.* II, 72).[35] According to Antoninus (570) it was the first station from Raphia to Pelusium *(al-Farama)*. The diocese was reestablished in 1996 with the consecration of Bishop Macari and was split in two after his death in 2000. Bishop Quzman was consecrated in 2001 for al-Arish and northern Sinai and Bishop Apollo was consecrated for al-Tur and southern Sinai.

Aswan *(Syene)*. Bishop Nilammon (fourth century) and Bishop Hadra (fifth century) are well known. The monastic settlements were visited by St. Pachomius (fifth century) *Syene* was always a bishopric. Bishop Hadra was consecrated in June 1975 for Aswan and Edfu *(Apollonos Megale* or *Apollonopolis)*, an ancient Episcopal See, that suffered during the eleventh century Nubian incursions.

Asyut *(Lycopolis)*. Center for the martyrdoms of Thecla, Claudius, Pamoun, Serne, Iskhiron of Qallin, Phoebammon, and Buqtur of Shu. Lycopolis became the center of the Meletian schism between Bishop Melitus and Pope Peter I regarding the issues following the Diocletian persecutions. Constantine II was an important bishop of the sixth century, a contemporary of Ephraim of Huw and Bisenti of Armant. The names of the bishops of Asyut are recorded. In the seventeenth century Bishops John and Paul also served Manfalut and Abu Tig. Metropolitan Mikhail was consecrated in August 1946.

Balyana. In the ninth century an Arian bishop of Balyana was excommunicated by Pope Shenute II (859–881). The diocese was reestablished in June 1975 with the consecration of Bishop Wisa.

Benha. This diocese was established in June 1992 with the consecration of Bishop Maximus to serve Benha and Quweisna.

Beni Mazar and al-Bahnasa *(Oxyrhynchos, Pemdje, Nea Justinou polis).* Famous for its saints Dermatheos, Apa Eliya, Apa Harmina, Apa Hor, Apa Ibsada, Apa Kolluthos, Bishop Latson, and the seventeen martyrs of Pemdje. An Episcopal See since the fourth century. Famous fourth-century bishops include Theodosius, Pelagius, Dionysius, Theodoros, Apollonios, and Apphon. In the fifth century there were twenty thousand nuns and ten thousand monks in the region. The bishops were registered from the tenth through eighteenth centuries. Prior to 2001 part of the bishopric of Beni Suef, was reinstated with the consecration of Bishop Athanasius in November 2001.

Beni Suef. A Christian community is recorded in the seventeenth century. In the nineteenth century the bishop resided in nearby Bush. In the middle of the twentieth century Metropolitan Athanasius of Beni Suef and al-Bahnasa (1962–2000) played an important role during the papacies of Cyril VI and Shenuda III. His successor, Bishop Ghobrial, was consecrated in June 2001.

Dair Mawas. This diocese was established in November 1988 with the consecration of Bishop Aghabius.

Dairut and Sanabu *(Senoabis)*. Sanabu, an old Episcopal See, famous for Bishop Menas of Sanabu (eighth century). In June 1986 Bishop Barsum was consecrated for the diocese.

Damanhur *(Hermopolis Mikra)*. Used to be the administrative center and Episcopal See of Chora Alexandreon. Its fourth-century martyrs were Apa Kyros, Ptolemaeos, Filya, and Apa Shenoufe. The Chora was famous for its convent with three hundred nuns and its role as dependency for the monastery of St. Jeremiah at Saqqara. In the eleventh century it served as dependency for the Monastery of St. Macarius. The medieval bishops are recorded, some of them served also Minufiya and Buhaira. Metropolitan Pachomius was consecrated in September 1990 and serves the city, the Tahrir province and the cities of the Pentapolis (Berenice, Arsinoë-Tauchira, Ptolemais, Cyrene, and Apollonia).

Dishna. The bishopric was established in May 1991 with the consecration of Bishop Takla.

Fashn *(Pbesin)*. The site for the Coptic legend of Aur and his brothers. The diocese, including Biba, was established in June 2001 with the consecration of Bishop Istefanus.

Fayyum *(Arsinoë)*. Bishop Nepos served the city in the third century. Some of the martyrs of the city were Apa Elia, Ibsada, and Kaw. Some of the fifth-century bishops were followers of Melitus. In the seventh century, many Christians of the region suffered persecution by the Chalcedonians, especially by Muqauqis, ruler of Egypt at the time of the Arab conquest. In 1243 there were thirteen monasteries and twenty-five churches in the region of Fayyum. From 1881 to 1914 the famous and charismatic Abra'am served as bishop. He was buried in Dair al-Azab. The new Bishop Abra'am was consecrated in June 1985.

Girga. An old Episcopal See. In the seventeenth century the bishop of Girga also served Naqada, Abu Tig, and Asyut. Bishop Mina is one of the oldest bishops.

Giza. In the eleventh century Ezekiel was Bishop of Giza and Ausim. In the twelfth century the island of Roda was part of Giza with the famous church of St. Mark. Since June 1985, Mutran Dumadius has been responsible for Giza.

Helwan and Ma'sara. Toward the end of September, many pilgrims from Cairo gather for the *mulid* of Barsum the Naked at Ma'sara. In the fourteenth century Pope John VIII (1300–1320) and Mark IV (1348–1568) came from Ma'sara. St. Barsum's church and monastery were rebuilt by Bishop Bisanti, who was consecrated in June 1988.

Hurghada. This bishopric was established in June 1992 with the consecration of Bishop Tawfilus to serve the Red Sea region.

Ismailiya. This bishopric was established in June 2001 with the consecration of Bishop Seraphim.

Kafr al-Shaikh *(Sakha, Xois)*. An ancient Christian city recorded on the famous sixth-century Madaba map mosaic (Madaba, Jordan). Episcopal See in the fourth century. Bishop Macedonius of Xois was present at the ecumenical council of Ephesus in 431. It is the city of St. Agathon the Stylite (seventh century). The Holy Family is believed to have stayed in Sakha, where a 'footprint of Jesus' was discovered in 1984. The metropolitan Bishai, Secretary of the Holy Synod, is bishop of the city and the Convent of St. Damiana at Bilqas.

Luxor. A new Episcopal See which includes the monasteries of St. George at al-Rizaiqat and that of St. Pachomius at Minshat al-Ammari. The bishopric includes Armant and Esna and was established in June 1976.

Maadi and Dar al-Salam. Established as a bishopric in June 1990 with the consecration of Bishop Daniel.

Maghagha. Established as a bishopric in November 2001 with the consecration of Bishop Agathon.

Mahalla al-Kubra *(Saire)*. This is the birthplace of Apa Paphnutius and Pope Cyril the Great (412–444). In the ninth century Pope Shenute II (859–882) used to stay at Mahalla. In the thirteenth century Bishop John served Mahalla and Sandafa. Bishop Matthias of Mahalla al-Kubra was consecrated in June 1989 and suspended in 2004.

Mallawi and Ashmunain *(Hermopolis Magna)*. Bishop Kolon (260) was bishop of Hermopolis (Euseb, HE VI, 46, 2).[36] Several bishops of the city were Melitians. Fifth-century tradition says the Holy Family visited Hermopolis in the first century. Full lists of bishops since the eighth century exist. The most famous bishop was Sawirus ibn al-Muqaffa', author of the *History of the Patriarchs of the Coptic Church*. In the thirteenth century Ashmunain was joined with the oases Taha, Minyat Abu Fis, and later with Qusqam (al-Qusiya). Bishop Demetrius was consecrated in June 1986.

Manfalut. In the sixteenth century it was known for its strong Christian population. Birthplace of Pope John XIV (1571–1586). In the eighteenth century Bishop John also served Asyut. Famous bishops were Abraham (1818) and Athanasius (1844). Bishop Antonius was consecrated in June 1986.

Mansura. Founded in 1218 by the Ayubid Sultan Malik al-Kamil at the time of the fifth crusade to Damietta. In the nineteenth century fifteen thousand Copts resided in the city. Bishop Dawud was consecrated on November 2002 as bishop of Mansura.

Matai. A new Episcopal See established with the consecration of Bishop Georgius in June 2001.

Minya. Founded by a Christian, ibn Khasib after whom the city was named. In the Middle Ages, there were eleven churches in Minya. In 1844 Bishop Yaqubus of Minya also served Ashmunain. Bishop Arsanius was consecrated in June 1976 for Minya and Abu Qurqas.

Minufiya. In June 1976 Bishop Banyamin was consecrated for the See of Minufiya.

Nag' Hammadi. Not mentioned prior to 1864, famous for the discovery of the collection of Gnostic papyri in 1954. The diocese was established with the consecration of Bishop Kyrillus in June 1977.

Naqada and Qus *(Diocletianopolis)*. An old bishopric, famous for Pisrael of Qus (fifth century), Apater of Qus (eleventh century), and Abraham of Qus (1844). The sixteenth century bishop Basilius (1580–1483) was born in Naqada. Bishop Bimen, consecrated in June 1991, serves both cities.

Old Cairo (Babylon, Fustat). Bishop Yuhanna has served this See since June 1991.

Port Said. A new Episcopal See served by Bishop Tadros since November 1976.

Qena and Qift *(Kainepolis)*. A bishopric since the nineteenth century. Well-known bishops are Mutran Luqa (1930) and Sharubim (2001).

Qusiya *(Koussai, Qusqam)*. A fourth-century bishopric served by orthodox and Melitian bishops. Bishop Theonas of Koussai attended the fifth ecumenical council in Constantinople. According to tradition, the Holy Family stayed at Qusqam. Bishops of Qusiya served Ashmunain, Taha, Abu Fis, and Sanabu in the period between the fourteenth and nineteenth centuries. Bishop Thomas of al-Qusiya and Meir was consecrated in November 1988.

Samalut *(Semolo)*. Known for its many fourth-century martyrs. Birthplace of Pope Mihail III (1477–1478). It served as dependency to the Monastery of Phoebammon near Hermopolis Magna. Bishop Paphnutius was consecrated in June 1976 to serve the diocese of Samalut.

Sharqiya. Bishop Angelus was consecrated in November 1976 to serve in the Province of Sharqiya.

Shibin al-Qanatir. According to a local tradition, the Holy Family stopped at Leontopolis, two kilometers northwest of Shibin al-Qanatir, where the Jews had established the temple of Onias IV, built on the model of the Jerusalem temple. Bishop Pisoura suffered martyrdom in this city (Tut 9). In June 1992, Bishop Samuel was consecrated to serve the diocese.

Shubra al-Khema or Shubra Damanhur. In the twelfth century the city was served by a married bishop! The city was once famous for the ritual of taking the relics of St. John of Sanhut, known for their healing powers, which are said to have left the reliquary to bathe in the nearby water and then returned to the church. Pope Gabriel II ibn Turaiq (1131–1145) prohibited the ceremony, which, however, was later resumed. In the twelfth century Shubra Damanhur was a bishopric. The bishopric was re-established with the consecration of Bishop Marcus in June 1992.

Sohag *(Suhay, Sumay)* developed in the nineteenth century. It is important because of the nearby White and Red Monasteries. Bishop Bakhum of Sohag was consecrated in June 1986.

Suez *(Clysma)* is a new Episcopal See. Bishop Ignatius was consecrated in May 1977.

Tahta *(Toeto)* was a center of Melitian theology (fifth century). Bishop Ishaia of Tahta was consecrated in June 1980.

Tanta. The See of Gharbiya was established in 1975 with the consecration of Bishop Yuhannes. Bishop Bula of Tanta was consecrated in 1989.

Tima. The martyrs of Tima are Apa Bigus, Apa Bifam, and Apa Bulus of Tima. The patron of the city is Abu Fam. Bishop Fam was consecrated in June 1980 to serve Tima.

Tur, Southern Sinai. This Episcopal See was established with the consecration of Bishop Apollo in June 2001.

Zaqaziq and Minya al-Qamh. A new diocese which was established with the consecration of Bishop Yaqubus in May 1977.

The British Orthodox Church of the Coptic Orthodox Patriarchate

The British Orthodox Church originated in 1866 with the consecration of Jules Ferrette as Bishop of Iona[37] by an oriental orthodox hierarch. In the past the church received its "apostolic authority" from various *episcopi vagantes*—clergy who claim priestly or episcopal orders via certain indisputably recognized bishops (Catholic or Orthodox). These clergy broke with those authorities and later consecrated bishops of their own. The theology of this community varied over the past century from the acceptance of the three, four, or seven ecumenical councils.

On June 4, 1994, William Henry Hugo Newman-Norton, once deacon, priest, and metropolitan of the British Orthodox Church, entered the Coptic Monastery of the Syrians in the Wadi al-Natrun as a monk. There he was anointed and on June 19, 1994, he was consecrated as Metropolitan Seraphim al-Suriani of Glastonbury.[38]

The British Orthodox church is a diocese of the Coptic Orthodox Patriarchate of Alexandria with jurisdiction over the United Kingdom, Republic of Ireland, the Isle of Man, and the Channel Islands. The church celebrates Easter according to the Gregorian calendar and uses the Liturgy of St. James (unknown to the Copts). The Coptic Orthodox dioceses in Great Britain remain distinct from the British Orthodox Church. The British Orthodox Church has ten parishes in England and one in Australia, served by seven priests and three deacons. The residence of H.E. Seraphim of Glastonbury is in London.

The French Coptic Orthodox Church

On Sunday June 2, 1974, Pope Shenouda instituted the Coptic Orthodox diocese of France, and consecrated the Dutch theologian Jan Frederik Nico Blom van Assendelft as its first bishop and the Frenchman Athanasius as his assistant bishop. On Sunday June 19, 1994, Bishop Marcos was consecrated metropolitan of France and Athanasius became bishop.[39] The residence of the French Coptic Orthodox Diocese is at 83200 Le Resest-Les-Eaux with the Church of Our Lady of Zeitun and the House of Our Lady of Scetis.

The French Coptic Orthodox Church has thirteen parishes, served by fourteen priests. In addition, the Church maintains two Coptic Orthodox Cultural Centers in Venice (Italy) and Porto (Portugal).

Coptic Monasticism

The Coptic Orthodox Church is essentially a monastic organization. The canons prescribe that the leadership of the church, the pope, the metropolitans, and the bishops are selected from the desert fathers. It is no oversimplification, therefore, to say that the state and the spirituality of the Coptic monasteries reflects and determines the state and the spirituality of the church, the dioceses, and the parishes. It also means that the future of the Coptic Orthodox Church lies solely in the future of its monastic movement. This was and is clearly understood by the late Pope Cyril VI (1959–1971) and Pope Shenuda III. It was no casual accident that the revival of the Coptic Orthodox Church in the mid-twentieth century coincided with the rejuvenation of the monasteries on account of many Sunday school teachers who had followed the call for a full and life-time service for the church.[40] For an understanding of the spiritual significance, there is no better way than to cite the pledge of initiation for becoming a monk.[41]

> I acknowledge that monasticism is a complete death to the world and all that is in it in the way of wealth and possessions, and in the way of relatives and friends, and in the way of appointments and occupations, and that it is a life of worship and dedication to God, a life of penitence and deprivation and perfect obedience and exclusion and poverty. And before God and His Angels and His Holy Altar,[42] and in the saintly presence of my father, the bishop, head of the monastery, and of the assembly of my fathers, the monks, members of this holy congregation, I dedicate my life to God, that I may live in virginity and contingency and estrangement from the world, promising that I will follow the life of true monasticism and obey its canons and its instructions, even as our saintly fathers have set for us, who have followed this angelic manner of life; even as I promise before God and His Angels and His Holy Altar and before all my fathers, that I will live in perfect obedience and submission to my fathers, the head of this monastery and his steward . . . even as I promise that I will not murmur and I will not abandon any work which they have entrusted to me. I will obey my father confessor with perfect obedience, and I will not do anything without his advice, and I will not conceal from him anything in the way of my sins and my deeds, and in the way of my thoughts and my feelings. . . . I will live a life of fellowship in the monastery, and I will not have any money of my own, and that, If God wills for me that I should live the life of solitude (eremitical), I will not do this without the advice of my father confessor. Even as I promise that I will not solicit any appointment in the world and wander about in it (as itinerant monk), and I will not solicit the ranks of the Priesthood. . . . If I transgress any article of these promises, I shall be unfitted for this angelic rank and worthy of any punishment imposed upon me. May the Lord grant that I may follow this way according to His goodness.[43]

Throughout the past fifty years, there has been an unprecedented increase of monks and nuns in the Coptic monasteries and convents, and the number of monastic institutions is still growing. While some of the new monasteries have been fully accredited by the Holy Synod, others are occupied by merely one or two monks since it is the policy of the church that many of the once-abandoned and partly ruined monastic buildings should be restored and subsequently be reoccupied. The following list presents both the officially accredited as well as some of the recently reoccupied monasteries.[44]

The **Monastery of the Romans *(Dair al-Baramus)***. The northernmost monastery of the four Wadi al-Natrun monasteries; the earliest settlement is thought to be around AD 340.

The **Monastery of St. Macarius *(Dair Abu Maqar)***. The southernmost monastery of the group, founded by St. Macarius the Great toward the middle of the fourth century. During the Middle Ages it served as pontifical residence.

The **Monastery of St. Bishoi *(Dair Anba Bishoi)***. It was founded by St. Bishoi toward the beginning of the fifth century. Since 1971 it has served as the desert residence for Pope Shenuda III.

The **Monastery of the Syrians *(Dair al-Surian)***. Dedicated to the Holy Virgin and St. John Kame, founded in the sixth century as a Theotokos monastery of St. Bishoi, it was acquired by Syrian monks in the eighth century, where they remained until the middle of the seventeenth century.

The **Monastery of St. Menas *(Dair Abu Mina)*** at Maryut, fifteen kilometers southeast of Burg al-'Arab, was founded in the fourth century and gained fame for its baths. The new monastery was dedicated in 1961 by Pope Cyril VI. His tomb is under the main altar.

The **Monastery of St. George *(Dair Mari Girgis)*** at Khatatba, Minufiya, was established in 1994 in response to the growing need for a monastery in Lower Egypt.

The **Monastery of Patmos**. The most recent addition to monastic life in Lower Egypt was founded in 1996 by H.G. Bishop Butrus. It is situated on the desert highway connecting Heliopolis and Suez (kilometer forty).

The **Monastic Dependencies of the Wadi al-Natrun Monasteries**: for the Dar al-Baramus the dependency is in Tukh Dalaka, Minufiya. The dependency for the Monastery of Saint Bishoi is at Kafr Daud near al-Terrana. The dependency for the Monastery of Abu Maqar is at Atris near Beni Salama. There is also the dependency for the Monastery of the Syrians.

The **Monastery of St. Antony *(Dair Anba Antunius)*** at Mt. Clysma in the Eastern Desert was founded between 361 and 363; in the late Middle Ages it provided many popes and the leadership of the Coptic and Ethiopian church.

The **Monastery of St. Paul the Theban *(Dair Anba Bula)*** was founded in memory of the first hermit in the fourth century, and existed most of the time in the shadow of St. Antony's Monastery. The dependencies of the two monasteries of the eastern desert are situated in the village of Bush, one hundred and twenty kilometers south of Cairo, in the district of Beni Suef.

The monasteries of the Fayyum region include the **Monastery of St. Gabriel *(Dair Malak Ghobrial)*** at Naqlun, which has profited from the recent monastic revival. The **Monastery of St. George *(Dair Mari Girgis)*** at Sidmant is twenty-five kilometers south of Medinat al-Fayyum. The **Monastery of the Holy Virgin and the Dove *(Dair al-Hammam)***, near the village of al-Lahun, is one of the recently (1985) reoccupied monasteries. The **Monastery of St. Samuel *(Dair Anba Samwil)*** in the desert of al-Qalamun, south of Fayyum, has benefited significantly from the recent monastic renaissance. The Laura of Wadi al-Rayan, south of Fayyum, once occupied by Father Matta al-Maskin from 1958 to 1969, was reoccupied by Father Ilisha' with seventeen monks in 1997.[45] **The Monastery of the Holy Virgin *(Dair al-Muharraq)***. Established by St. Pachomius, or his successor in the fifth century, it is regarded as the final destination of the Holy Family's flight to Egypt. It is known for its large *mulid* from June 21–28. Among the once abandoned monasteries east of Asyut, the **Monastery of St. Menas *(Dair Abu Mina)*** near Abnub has been reactivated.

The famous Upper Egyptian **Monastery of St. Shenute,** or the **White Monastery *(Dair al-Abiad)***, dates from the fourth century. In June 1997, it was officially recognized by the Holy Synod as the fifteenth Coptic monastery. On the edge of the desert east of Akhmim, the following once abandoned monasteries have been reestablished, the **Monastery of St. Thomas *(Dair Abu Tuma)*** east of al Salamuni; the **Monastery of St. Michael *(Dair al-Malak)***; the **Monastery of the Martyrs *(Dair al-Shuhada)***, the **Monastery of the Holy Virgin *(Dair al-'Adhra)***– all of them east of al-Hawawish. Moreover, there are the **Monastery of St. George *(Dair Mari Girgis al-Hadidi)*** and the **Monastery of St. Pisada *(Dair Apa Bisada)*** at al-Ahaiwa Sharq. These monasteries are being reactivated, the largest one being the **Monastery of the Martyrs**.

Further south on the highway between Nag' Hammadi and Qena, there is the **Monastery of St. Palemon *(Dair Anba Balamun)***, a Pachomian foundation, now being reactivated. Eight kilometers northeast of the ruins of the Temple of Karnak in Luxor is the **Monastery of St. Pachomius *(Dair Anba Bakhum)***, officially recognized in June 1997. South of Luxor and southeast of Armant is the **Monastery of St. George *(Dair Mari Girgis)*** at al-Riziqat. This monastery was reoccupied in 1976. The popular mulid at this monastery takes place between November 10–16. The **Monastery of St. Matthew the Potter *(Dair Anba Matta)***, founded in the eighth century, is situated in Nag' al-Zinaiqa, seven kilometers west of Asfun. This monastery was reoccupied in 1975. The **Monastery of St. Pachomius *(Dair Anba Bakhum)*** west of Edfu, for many centuries unoccupied, was rebuilt and reoccupied in 1975. Next to the seventh-century **Monastery of St. Simeon *(Dair Anba Sama'an)*** opposite Aswan, Bishop Hadra of Aswan has recently built a new monastery, since the former building now belongs to the Antiquities Department.

The Convents of Nuns

Parallel to the establishment of new monastic communities, partly by reactivating once abandoned and unoccupied monasteries, Coptic nuns have also repeopled some of the former monastic settlements, especially in Upper Egypt. The following convents are presently active. The **Convent of St. Damiana *(Dair Sitt Dimyana)***, recently part of the diocese of Kafr al-Shaikh *(Sakha)*, has been a monastery and pilgrimage site since the Middle Ages. The monastery was rededicated by Pope Shenuda III in May 1975 for nuns. Since 1981, the convent also serves as center for the deaconesses *(shammasa)*.

In Cairo there are five convents: the **Convent of the Holy Virgin *(Dair al-'Adhra)*** and that of **St. George *(Dair Mari Girgis)*** are in Harat Zuwailah. The **Convent of St. Theodore *(Dair Amir Tadrus)*** is in Harat al-Rum. Two convents are in Old Cairo, that of **St. Mercurius *(Dair Abu al-Saifain)*** and that of **St. George *(Dair Mari Girgis)***. The history of these five convents can be traced to the Middle Ages.

The **Convent of the Daughters of St. Mary *(Banat Maryam)*** in Beni Suef was founded by the Metropolitan Athanasius in 1965. It was only after two years of preparation that this community was ultimately recognized by Pope Cyril VI as "a community of active nuns," since 1970 instituted as "consecrated women" *(makarrasat)* to distinguish them from nuns. Nuns lead a strict contemplative life within the walls of their convents, often surpassing the ascetic practices of the monks. "Consecrated women" are also celibate but are active in the community in dioceses and parishes. "Consecrated women" could join as virgins but also as widows. Some Coptic nuns live at the Monastery of Durunka, ten kilometers south of Asyut, assisting at the time of the *mulid* between August 7–22 in commemoration of the Assumption of the Holy Virgin and the Flight of the Holy Family.

The **Convent of St. Theodore *(Dair al-Shahid Tadrus al-Muharib)*** is situated in the desert around five hundred meters southwest of the temple of Medinet Habu on the west bank of the Nile, south of Luxor. This convent was reactivated in 1975. South of Luxor, on the east bank of the Nile, is the village of Tud with the **Convent of St. Pisentius *(Dair Anba Bisenti)***, which was occupied in the 1970s. The southernmost Coptic convent is dedicated to **St. Ammonius *(Dair Apa Amun)***, six kilometers southwest of Esna on the edge of the desert. According to tradition, the site was consecrated by Pope Peter I in the fourth century. These nuns offer special veneration to St. Dulagi and her four sons, who suffered martyrdom during the Decian persecution.

The Orthodox Emigration and the Coptic Orthodox Churches Overseas

Emigration has become in the past half century an alternative for Copts to escape domestic problems, including economical hardship, discrimination, and sometimes violence. In the 1960s, the first Coptic Orthodox churches were founded in Germany and in England. Soon Copts crossed the Atlantic to settle in the United States and Canada, while others crossed the Pacific and established churches in Australia and New Zealand.

In the United States there are one hundred and twenty-five Coptic Orthodox churches, served by one hundred and sixty-three parish priests. These are:

The **Archdiocese of North America** in Cedar Grove, New Jersey (Bishop David) includes the Diocese of Los Angeles, Southern California, and Hawaii (Bishop Serapion), and the Diocese of the Southern United States (Bishop Youssef) in Colleyville, Texas.

The **Diocese of Los Angeles, Southern California, and Hawaii** has twenty-four parishes with forty-one priests in Anaheim, Bakersfield, Bellflower, Cathedral City, Colton, Covina, Lake Forest, Los Angeles, Moorpark, Norco, Northridge, Orange County, Palm Springs, Palmdale, Pomona, Salana Beach, Santa Anna, Santa Clara, Santa Monica, Torrance, Victorville, and Visalia; Hawaii: Honolulu.

The **Diocese of the Southern United States** includes thirty-three parishes with forty-two priests in Alabama: Birmingham, Mobile; Arizona: Scottsdale, Tucson; Florida: Clearwater, Daytona Beach, Destan, Fort Myers, Jacksonville, Oviedo, Pompano Beach, Sarasota, Talahassee, Tampa; Georgia: Roswell; Louisiana: Lafayette, New Orleans, Shraveport; New Mexico: Albuquerque; Nevada: Las Vegas; Oklahoma: Oklahoma City, Tulsa; Tennessee: Chattanooga, Knoxville, Memphis, Nashville; Texas: Bellaire, College Station, Colleyville, Richardson, Houston, Lubbock, and San Antonio. The Coptic Orthodox Monastery of St. Antony is in Yermo, California.

The following sixty-eight parishes with eighty priests are listed alphabetically by state. California: Campbell, Concord, Fresno, Hayward, Modesto, Presidio of Monterey, Rancho Cordova; Colorado: Englewood; Connecticut: Hamden; Delaware: Bear; Illinois: Burr Ridge, Troy; Minnesota: South St. Paul; Missouri: St. Louis; Nebraska: Omaha; New Jersey: Bayonne, Cherryhill, East Brunswick, East Rutherford, Holmdel, Howell, Jersey City, McKee City; New York: Albany, Astoria, Brooklyn, North White Plains, Ridgewood, Rochester, Spring Valley, Staten Island, Syracuse, Woodbury; North Carolina: Charlotte, Raleigh, N. Myrtle Beach, Columbus, Miamisburg, Seven Hills, Toledo; Oregon: Portland; Pennsylvania: Ambridge, Annville, Philadelphia, Silver Spring; Rhode Island: Cranston; South Carolina: Greenville; Virginia: Fairfax, Richmond, Williamsburg; Washington: Lynnwood, Puyallup, Seattle; West Virginia: Huntington; and Wisconsin: Waterford. The Pope Shenuda III Theological Seminary is in Cedar Grove, New Jersey.

In **Canada** there are twenty-seven parishes with forty priests in Alberta: Calgary, Edmonton; British Columbia: Surrey; Manitoba: Winnipeg, New Brunswick, St. Hubert; Nova Scotia: Halifax; Ontario: Ajax, Barrie, Brampton, Etobicoke, Gloucester, Hamilton, Kingston, Kitchener, London, Mississaugam Napean, North York, Toronto, St. Catherine, York, Windsor, Quebec: Montreal, Pierrefonds, Quebec City, St. Hubert.

In **Central and South America** there are four parishes with three priests. They are in Bolivia: Santa Cruz; Brazil: Sao Paulo; Bermuda: Hamilton; Virgin Islands: St. Thomas; St. Kitts, West Indies, Basseterre.

In **Central Europe** there are fifty-four parishes with forty-six priests.

In **Austria** (Bishop Gabriel): Vienna, Graz, and Linz.

Belgium: Brussels and Antwerp.

Cyprus: Limassol and Nicosia.

Denmark: Copenhagen.

France: Paris, Marseille, Villejuif, Ronchères, Deuil-la-Barre, and Asnières-sur-Seine.

Germany (Bishop Damian) Höxter, Berlin, Bielefeld, Bonn, Bremen, Dortmund, Düsseldorf, Frankfurt, Hamburg, Hannover, Kröffelbach, Mürnberg, Stuttgart, and Trier.

Greece: Athens.

Italy: Diocese of Milan (Bishop Kyrillus), Milan; Diocese of Turin (Bishop Barnabas) Rome, Florence, and Turin.

The Netherlands: Amsterdam, The Hague, Eindhoven, Utrecht, Leeuwarden, and Assen.

Spain: Cervera.

Sweden: Stockholm and Gothenburg.

Switzerland: Geneva, Zürich, Basel, Biel, and Lugano.

In the **United Kingdom** there are seventeen parishes with seventeen priests. The Diocese of Birmingham (Bishop Misail): Lapworth, Warwickshire; Birmingham; and Nottingham. The Diocese of Scotland, Ireland, and North England (Bishop Anthony): Doncaster; Newcastle; Norwich; and Margate, Kent. Ireland: Co-Wicklow. Scotland: Kirkcaldery, Fife. Diocese of England (Bishop Anglos): Stevenage, Hertfordshire; London; Croydon; Brighton; and Manchester. Wales: Newport, Gwent.

In **Australia and New Zealand** there are thirty-seven parishes with sixty-nine priests. The Diocese of Melbourne (Bishop Suriel), Mitcham North, Victoria; Australian Capital Territory: Kaleen, ACT; South Australia: Adelaide, SA; Victoria: Oakleigh, VIC, Heathcote, Bulleen, St. Albans, Preston, Kensington, Hallam, and Donavle; Tasmania: Newstead; Western Australia: East Victoria Park and Wanneroo. The diocese of 'Sydney and its Affiliated Regions' (Bishop Daniel) includes New South Wales (Mt. Druitt, Long Point, Guildford, Punchbowl, Kensington, Liverpool, Arncliffe, Kirrawee, Rhodes, Newcastle, Wagga Wagga, Penrith, Bexley, Dural, Collaroy, Blacktown), Queensland (Brisbane, Gold Coast), and Northern Territory (Darwin) in Australia, as well as Japan, Thailand, and Singapore. The Coptic communities in these countries are too small to have their own dioceses. The Pope Shenuda III Theological College is in Arncliffe, NSW; the St. Athanasian Theological College is in Donville, VIC. The other Coptic Colleges are in Mt. Druitt, Wattle Grove, Beuxley and Frankstone North, VIC. The St. Shenuda the Archimandrite Monastery is in Putty, NSW, the Monastery of St. Anthony is in Heathcote, VIC. New Zealand: Auckland, Christchurch, and Dunedin.

In sub-Saharan **Africa** there are twenty-four parishes and twenty-one priests assisted by several deacons. The Diocese of Khartoum and North Sudan (Bishop Iliya), Khartoum. The Diocese of Omdurman (Bishop Sarabamun), Omdurman. The Bishopric of African Affairs (Bishop Antonius Marcus), Johannesburg, South Africa serves ten churches in South Africa, four in Orange Free States, two in Kwa Zulu Natal, one each in East Cape, Western Cape, and Durban. Churches are maintained in Abidjan, Ivory Coast, in Lubumbashi, Democratic Republic of the Congo; in Accra, Ghana; in Ondangwa and Windhoek, Namibia; in Lome, Togo. The three African Coptic monasteries are: St. Anthony's Monastery in Nairobi, Kenya; St. Mina's Monastery in Luanda, Angola and St. Anthony's Monastery in Harare, Zimbabwe.

In the **Middle East** Metropolitan Abraham, Jerusalem, is responsible for the Coptic holy places in Jerusalem and Bethlehem, there are churches in Jerusalem, Bethlehem, Nazareth, Haifa, and Amman.

Issues of the Coptic Orthodox Inculturation in Western Societies

Due to their complexities only six aspects of these problems will be presented: the concept of inculturation; the Coptic identity in the countries of emigration by name, tattoo, language, and cultural belongingness; the ambivalence of Coptic aesthetics in the search for identity; the adherence to Coptic Orthodox doctrine as a means to preserve the communal identity; the Copts and their assessment of theological adiaphora, those matters of 'lesser importance'; and some thoughts about the maintenance of the Coptic identity in the countries of emigration.

The Concept of Inculturation

The theological usage of the concept of inculturation pertains to the relationship of the message of the Gospel and the institution of the respective church to the culture of a certain people. In view of the inherent tensions between the institutions of the church and the structures of society, both sides are naturally faced with a variety of reciprocal attitudes ranging from a sense of indifference to more or less acceptance and outright hostility.

Prototypical for the ecclesiastical process of inculturation is the biblical report of the Apostles' Council in Jerusalem (Acts 15). The messianic Jews of the Jerusalem congregation continued in their traditional Jewish practices and demanded that "it was needful to circumcise them [the Gentiles] and to command them to keep the law of Moses" (Acts 15:5). On the other hand, the Roman and Hellenistic new converts to the Christian faith considered the demand for circumcision as a sacrilegious act of self-mutilation, utterly unacceptable to them. Finally it was agreed that the Christian faith could be practiced within the cultural environment of the believers without adhering to the Mosaic prescriptions of the law as demanded by the 'Mother Church.'

> For it seemed good to the Holy Ghost, and to us, to lay upon you no greater burden than these necessary things; that ye abstain from meats offered to idols, and from blood, and from things strangled, and from fornication: from which if ye keep yourselves ye shall do well, Fare ye well.
>
> (Acts 15:28, 29; King James' Version)

The Coptic Identity in the Countries of Emigration

As a minority, the Copts are in many ways unique. At certain periods in the early Middle Ages every Egyptian Christian was compelled by the Islamic authorities to identify himself as a believer in Jesus Christ. He was obliged to wear, hanging from his neck, a heavy wooden cross. Today, the Copts carry simpler labels to assure their identity. In Egypt, more than in any other Middle Eastern country, the name of a person betrays his religious and ethnic identity. Coptic names are inclusive, and in addition to the ancient pharaonic names, the Copts have borrowed and transformed Greek, Latin, Hebrew-Aramaic, Ethiopian, Arabic, Syrian, French, and English names. Following the introduction of Christianity in the Nile Valley, an Egyptian who had accepted the Christian Faith selected Christian names, i.e., names of Biblical personages, Church Fathers, saints, monks, and hermits. Thus many Hebrew-Aramaic, Greek, and Latin names were introduced into Egypt. At the same time, many pre-Christian names were preserved, because their bearers, who were martyrs, saints or monks, had been canonized. This is especially true of many pharaonic names, such as Amun, Hor, and Sarabamun. It is amazing how many names of the pharaonic period have survived in the personal names of the Copts. During the Hellenistic, Roman, and Byzantine eras, Greek and Latin names were widely adopted by the Copts. After the Arab conquest, Coptic and Greek names were often translated into Arabic, for example Christodoulus into *Abd al-Masih*. During the French, and particularly during the British occupation, numerous Copts gave their children Western names, such as Cromer, Kitchener, Henry, and William. While in Egypt there is a trend toward religiously neutral names, in the countries of emigration, Copts largely follow the name-giving customs of their new environment.[46]

With a certain sense of pride many Copts still point to the cross tattooed on the inside of their right wrist. In Western society—for a certain group of people—the usage of tattoos has become a rather widespread fashionable craze, although completely unrelated to any religious significance. On the other hand, for the Copts the tattoo of the cross or any other Christian symbol represents a visible and permanent testimony to their faith in Jesus Christ. Since the custom of the religious tattoo is dependent upon the cultural environment, it is a problem for the Copts in the countries of emigration. It is a question as to whether these Copts are prepared to continue this age-old Christian custom. It is much more likely that Copts visiting Egypt will attend one or the other *mulid* in honor of the Holy Virgin or one of the popular saints. At this occasion they may then resort to a tattooer. Usually he sets up his booth near the church and offers a variety of cross designs and pictures of the Holy Virgin or one of the equestrian saints. Nowadays the tattoos are applied with an electric needle.

The problem of Coptic linguistic identity has been an issue ever since the early Middle Ages. There are five Coptic dialects: Sa'idic, Bohairic, Fayyumic, Akhmimic, and Subakhmimic. Of these dialects only Bohairic is in use as the liturgical language of the Coptic Church. Although Sa'idic was the general Coptic language until the ninth century, Bohairic replaced it, partly on account of ecclesiastical influence. Already in the twelfth century, Pope Gabriel II (1131) admonished the priests for reciting the Lord's Prayer in vernacular Arabic rather than the liturical language of Bohairic. In the thirteenth and fourteenth centuries, Coptic liturgical books begin to have an Arabic translation side by side with the Coptic. Yet in Upper Egypt, Coptic seems to have prevailed much longer. Al-Maqrizi (fifteenth century) implies that Coptic was still spoken in the monasteries around Asyut. It is generally believed that Coptic ceased to be a spoken language in the seventeenth century.[47]

In Egypt Arabic is the accepted means of communication. It is true, in some urban upper-class circles ladies used to converse in French, the men in English. In the countries of emigration, however, the Copts are forced to employ the language of their selected country. While the first generation of emigrants may continue to speak Arabic, their children and grandchildren communicate in their adoptive language. In both the United States and Australia (Sydney, Los Angeles, and New York), Coptic schools are being established "in order to bring up the new generation of our children in a pure and academic atmosphere, away from any undesirable influences."[48] In these institutions, classes in Coptic language, history, and doctrine are being offered. However, since Coptic is a dead language, the Coptic emigrants are in a considerably less favorable situation than their Italian, Greek, Armenian, and Spanish counterparts whose languages remain living vehicles of communication.

Ethnically the Copts believe themselves to be the true Egyptians, the sons and daughters of the pharaohs. Just as the Assyrian Christians in Mesopotamia consider themselves as heirs of Hammurabi and Assurbanipal, and the Lebanese Maronites believe that they are the successors of Hiram and Ithobal, so many Copts point with pride to their ancestry beginning with Menes, the founder of the First Dynasty in 2900 BC.

Whereas from a Biblical point of view the Copts, the Mizraim, were the grandchildren of Noah through Ham (Genesis 10:6), ethnically speaking they are North Africans. The use of the Arabic language identifies them with the pan-Arab world extending from the Atlantic to the Arabian Gulf. Moreover, they practice certain customs and share numerous values, tastes, and habits with the Muslim majority. In times of national crisis, the Copts have demonstrated their loyalty to the political aspirations of the government.

Regarding their political opinions, the Copts in the countries of emigration are naturally inclined to reflect the political and social atmosphere of their national environment, as they do in their homeland.

As Arabic-speaking Christians, the Copts share their faith in Jesus Christ and in many religious values with the other arabophone Christians of the Middle East, be they Orthodox, Catholic, or Protestant. Their active participation in the Middle East Council of Churches confirms this ecumenical endeavor.

The Ambivalence of Coptic Aesthetics in the Search for Identity

The use of icons and devotional prints in Coptic churches, homes, and offices is certainly not limited to Egypt. In fact, Coptic churches and homes in the countries of emigration are easily recognized by their typical Coptic devotional pictures. The Coptic publishing houses, for example Mahaba Bookshop in Shubra, provide a wide variety of Christian devotional material and artwork which is obtainable in the kiosks of most Coptic churches.[49]

Around the mid-1950s a new school of Coptic iconographic art emerged at the Higher Institute of Coptic Studies in Abbasiya. Under the leadership of Professor Isaac Fanus, a student of Léonide Ouspensky in Paris, a neo-Coptic style of Christian art was created, altogether different from traditional Western and Byzantine art. He and his students embellished many parish and monastic churches in Egypt, Europe, the United States, and Australia. Today, the foremost Coptic iconographers are: Mansur Farag; Yusuf Girgis Ayad; Kamilia Shawky; Bidor Latif; Youssef Nassif; the Reverend Fathers Maksimus and Bishoi of Monastery of Saint Antunius;

Yusab and Samwil of Monastery of the Syrians; Elias of the Monastery of Baramus; and Arsanius of Monastery of Saint Bula. It has been pointed out that while Italian images of the Virgin's garments are portrayed in a bright, light blue, Coptic art prefers to show her in brown and indigo, since these colors were used by the ancient Coptic painters. Coptic figures are heavily outlined and give an almost severe impression. Typically, Coptic faces are round with large eyes and thick eyebrows.

In Coptic churches and homes of the emigration, this neo-Coptic art has been widely accepted, in spite of the fact that traditional Catholic and Byzantine objects of art have been readily available everywhere. It is of interest that in the emigration neo-Coptic icons have shown miraculous manifestations. Thus for example, Professor Fayek Ishaq reported the apparition of Christ on Friday evening, September 23, 1988 in the Coptic Orthodox Church of St. Mark, Agincourt, Ontario. Five Coptic maidens observed the icon of "Christ Seated in His Throne of Glory" by Bidor Latif and Youssef Nassif, which "was gradually transfigured and bathed in a dazzling flood of divine light; the whole scene looked three dimensional and the Lord's right hand moved upwards and downwards. . . ."[50] In May and again in August 1990 two neo-Coptic icons by Yussef Bishara (1979) in the Coptic Orthodox Church of St. Mark, Seven Hills, Cleveland, Ohio, issued oil. On May 15, 20, 22, and June 4, and again on August 24 and 26, the icon of the Holy Virgin with the Christ-child showed stains of oil on the neck. In case of the icon of Jesus Christ the oil also appeared on the neck of Christ. Bishop Tadros, Bishop of Port Said, who happened to be visiting Cleveland, testified to the miraculous issuance of oil.[51] These are noteworthy cases of inculturation. Faith in miraculous icons of Christ or the Holy Virgin is deeply entrenched in the Coptic consciousness. In the days of Patriarch Quzman (851–855) the icons in the monasteries of the Wadi al-Natrun began to weep because of the unjust walis and qadis. The same occurred in the days of Patriarch Christodoulus (1047–1077), though this time because of the sins of the Christians! This belief accompanied the emigrants to their new environment thereby testifying to their ancient religious and cultural heritage in the 'New World.'

An interesting case of inculturation took place on Monday, November 11, 1991 when the twelve-year-old Isaac Ayoub of Houston, Texas, suffering from leukemia, saw that the eyes of Jesus in the famous Sallman "Head of Christ" began moving and shedding an oily liquid like tears. On the same day, Father

Ishaq Soliman, the Coptic priest of St. Mark's Coptic Church in Houston, testified to the miracles. On the following day, Dr. Atef Rizkalla, the family physician, examined the youth and certified that there were no traces of leukemia. Sallman's "Head of Christ" was exhibited in the Coptic Church and more than fifty thousand people visited the church. Two Coptic bishops, Bishop Tadros of Port Said and Bishop Yuhanna of Cairo, verified the story. In this case, it was neither a Coptic icon nor a neo-Coptic print that served as a vehicle of the healing grace of God. The famous "Head of Christ" by the Protestant artist Warner E. Sallman (1892–1968) is by far the most popular Jesus picture in the US with more than five hundred million prints.[52]

While the modern Coptic artists have diligently decorated numerous churches in Egypt and offered their artwork in the form of prints at the various church kiosks, authentic studies have revealed that "the neo-Coptic images are not particularly popular. Their style creates a barrier . . . the stylized figures and postures, the lack of facial expression, the economy of details can be found artificial . . . there is a tendency to apprehend the popular images as being more beautiful than the neo-Coptic ones. . . . While the large group of users prefer the European and Byzantinesque images, artists of the neo-Coptic style regard many of the popularly preferred images as banal, gaudy and cheap."[53] These testimonies about devotional Coptic art reflect a rather interesting ambiguity as to the aesthetic norms of Egyptian Christians. I have shown that the popular iconography of the mariophanies of Zeitun in the spring of 1968 and of Ard Babadeblu, Shubra, in the spring of 1986 relied exclusively on a nineteenth-century Roman Catholic model, namely on the "Immaculata of the Miraculous Medallion." In July, November, and December 1830 the Holy Virgin appeared to Cathérine Labouré. Her vision of the Holy Virgin determined the Coptic iconography of the Cairo mariophanies.[54]

Today, the two most popular devotional prints which are distributed by the Copts from Alexandria to Aswan are the "Mater Dolorosa" by the Florentine master Carlo Dolci (1616–1686), and Guido Reni's "Ecce Homo" (1575–1642). Copies of these medieval Italian masterpieces are found in many Coptic churches and monasteries. Carlo Dolci's "Mater Dolorosa" has even become a Coptic cult image. According to Coptic tradition, on May 17, 1989, a poster of the "Mater Dolorosa" (85 x 55 centimeters) in the new Church of St. George in the village of Wadi al-Natrun showed signs of 'tears of blood.' Traces of this flow from her right eye over her cheek have remained visible on the picture.[55] In fact, the assertion of this 'miracle' demonstrates a significant sociopolitical indication. Only a few years after the glorious mariophanies of Zeitun (1968) and Ard Babadeblu (1986) with the image of the Immaculata, Coptic aesthetic taste reflected the new domestic situation for them and turned to a Holy Virgin of suffering and pain. Even the high relief decorating the Episcopal throne in the new Cathedral of the Holy Virgin of Zeitun in Tumambey Street shows Carlo Dolci's "Mater Dolorosa." And whatever has been said about the message of the "Mater Dolorosa" is also applicable to Guido Reni's "Ecce Homo" or "Man of Sorrows."[56]

Modern Coptic aesthetics in both Egypt and the emigration are dependent upon several factors. As we have seen, the sociopolitical climate in Egypt determines unwillingly the spiritual needs of the Christian minority. These are subsequently reflected in the collective aesthetics of the people. This also explains their attachment to the traditional pictures, be they Western or Byzantine. The situation in the countries of emigration is altogether different. Here, neo-Coptic art serves as a meaningful historical and existential bridge to the Coptic heritage on the banks of the Nile. As icons, sacred images contain the presence of the holy person portrayed, irrespective of the origin of the artist!

The Adherence to Coptic Doctrine as a Means to Preserve the Communal Identity

From a religious point of view the Orthodox Copts are oriental Christians like the Ethiopians, Syrians (Jacobites), Indians (Gacobites), and Armenians. They adhere to the famous Christological formula of St. Cyril of Alexandria "*Mia physis tou Theou Lógou sesarkoméne.*" From May 4–10, 1973, Pope Shenuda III, accompanied by eight Egyptian and two Ethiopian metropolitans, visited the Vatican where they were graciously received by Pope Paul VI. On this occasion the two pontiffs signed the document of agreement pertaining to the meaning of the Christological formula of St. Cyril of Alexandria, the "*mia physis.*" "Jesus Christ is perfect God with respect to His Divinity, perfect Man with respect to His Humanity. In Him His Divinity is united with His Humanity in a real perfect union without mingling, without separation and without division. In Him are preserved all the properties of His Divinity and all the properties if His

Humanity together in a real perfect indivisible Union." In October 1991 more than one hundred and twenty Roman Catholic and non-Chalcedonian (oriental) theologians gathered at the Monastery of Saint Bishoi to clarify and to end the historic and popular polemic, which for centuries had mistakenly accused the Copts of denying the human nature of Jesus Christ. Agreement was reached that the Christological mystery was expressed in different words and in different traditions, though adhering to the same fundamental faith.

Theologically the Copts are Biblical fundamentalists adhering to the doctrine of the verbal infallibility of the Holy Scriptures. They accept the teachings of the first three ecumenical councils of Nicea (325), Constantinople (381), and Ephesus (431), and those of the pre-Chalcedonian Fathers, Sts. Justin, Irenaeus, Clement of Alexandria, Hippolytus, Ephraem Syrus, Cyprian, and the three Cappadocian Fathers. They also accept the teachings of the Egyptian and Syrian post-Chalcedonian Fathers, like Severus of Antioch, James of Sarug, and the pontifical Alexandrian-Antiochene *synodica* of the ninth to the eleventh centuries. The Copts also hold to the canons of the seven, fourth, and fifth century synods of Anerya, Neocaesarea, Gangra, Antioch, Laodicea, Sardica, and Carthage. For their liturgical and disciplinary life they follow the thirty-one canons of Patriarch Gabriel II ibn Turaik (1131–1145) and the complete Canon Law by Patriarch Cyril III ibn Laqlaq (1235–1243). With respect to their strict adherence to the teachings of the Holy Scriptures, the Copts show certain affinities to some of the conservative evangelical churches, although the Coptic emphasis upon the Holy Virgin, the saints and their traditions in general, as well as their hierarchical structure, finds them more closely related to some of the Byzantine churches. In view of the plurality of churches in the countries of the emigration it is imperative that the Coptic Church provides regular seminars for the clergy and the laity. These should be under the auspices of the 'Office of Emigration Affairs' at the pontifical residence in Abbasiya.

The Copts and Their Assessment of Theological Adiaphora

In theory, all the canons of the ecumenical councils and synods are accepted as binding, except those prescribing ecclesiastical penalties which under the present circumstances cannot be enforced. At the same time, some of the canons were written in response to particular historical situations, and, therefore, are not applicable for all times. The canons of Cyril III are an exception. These form the basis of the Personal Status Laws.

The following few excerpts from the canons show that at least some of them must be regarded nowadays as adiaphora. According to the ninety-five canons of the Synod of Neocaesarea (350) priests should not be ordained until they have reached the age of thirty. The canons of Laodicea (343) prohibit Orthodox members marrying non-Orthodox ones or heretics, that members of the clergy should not enter taverns, and that beds should be set up in churches (probably for the sake of incubation). Moreover, they prohibit men and women bathing together. The one hundred and thirty-seven canons of Carthage (419) prohibit usury (interest-taking) by both priests and laymen. Those who communicate with the excommunicated are *ipso facto* excommunicated. The last canons also prohibit the practice of rebaptism.

Whereas the thirty-four canons of Cyril III demand that circumcision of boys be practiced prior to baptism, the Copts in the emigration, especially in Europe where this custom is quite uncommon, consider circumcision as an adiaphoron. Some of the Coptic fasting practices fall into the category of the adiaphora. There are some Copts who fast during the stipulated periods from sunrise to sunset, others only until 3 pm, while others again consider fasting as abstinence from animal products, with the exception of fish in all fasting periods other than Lent. Most Copts adhere to the Lenten fast (fifty-five days) and the Fast of the Holy Virgin (fifteen days), although in both cases not necessarily for the full period. For the Copts in the emigration the Christmas fast of forty-three days is extremely difficult because of the opulent Advent entertainments and festivities in Western society.

For the first time the Orthodox Copts live in a religiously pluralistic society which demands a profound sense of understanding of the democratic values of the individual. This pertains, for example, to the celebration of the Sacrament of Holy Matrimony of an Orthodox Copt with a non-Orthodox Coptic Christian, a Protestant, or a Roman Catholic, a situation that undoubtedly occurs quite often. According to present orthodox teaching and practice the Sacrament of Holy Matrimony can only be celebrated if both partners are Orthodox Copts. This means that a non-Orthodox Coptic Christian must be baptized and anointed before receiving the Holy Eucharist and subsequently be married.[57] In some communities a possible compromise has been reached by anointing the non-Orthodox Coptic Christian instead of rebaptism, which is difficult to administer because of lack of suitable adult baptisteries. At any rate, the Anabaptist practice of the Orthodox Copts has caused serious problems with both the Catholic and Protestant churches in the emigration. After all, the Sacrament of Holy Baptism performed with water and in the name of the Holy Trinity used to be considered as the one ecumenical means of grace.

On account of the new situation in Western society, theological and disciplinary prescriptions (not canons) have been set forth by Coptic churchmen in the emigration. The theological threats of fourth- and fifth-century Arianism, Nestorianism, or Donatism are no longer the pressing problem, but rather such movements as the Rosicrucians, Freemasons, Scientologists, Baghwan, Jehovah's Witnesses, and the Children of God. It is deemed that association with them should be avoided. Orthodox Copts also warn about such social and moral evils as gambling, rock music, fortune-telling, astrology, smoking, and dancing.[58] In an open society such ecclesiastical demands must be regarded as adiaphora.

On the Maintenance of Coptic Identity in the Emigration

Coptic emigration during the second half of the twentieth century is undoubtedly the most significant demographic movement in the history of the Coptic Church. The exodus had already begun in the late fifties, and continued throughout the sixties, seventies, eighties, and nineties on account of repressive political and economic measures. Already in 1963 Edward Wakin wrote:

> The attachment of the Copts to their Egyptian homeland is dramatized in the small-scale diaspora of the young, the educated and the qualified who have begun to leave Egypt. They leave with reluctance, talking not of greener pastures elsewhere but of closed doors at home. Feeling deprived of the traditional Coptic right to market their skills at a reasonably high price, they turn to the last resort of departure and dispersion. Yet the trappings of the Coptic identity are not suited to long journeys. Its symbols and ceremonies need the church and clergy which are left behind, while departure breaks he closed circle of community life.[59]

Wakin goes on to describe the situation of the emigrant Copt in the late 1950s:

> Copts, already Westernized, become invisible in a western country. In another Middle East country, they blend into the mosaic of Arab Christian minorities. If the Copt continues to attend church abroad, he will go to a Greek Orthodox Church or an Eastern Catholic Church. Sometimes he chooses a Protestant church.[60]

Wakin's description of the situation of the Copts in the emigration predates the establishment of the first Coptic congregation in the United States in 1968.[61] In the meantime more than thirty years have passed by and numerous Coptic churches have been founded to respond to the needs of the emigrant Copts. Professor Fayek Ishak has provided a very honest evaluation of the relationship of the emigrant Copt to his church: "It is regrettable that quite a number of Coptic families living abroad have left their church and joined non-Orthodox denominations. Others have given up the church altogether after the irritation and distraction caused by the stubborn accommodation of the elderly generation of churchgoers. No doubt we are responsible for bringing up groups of atheists who know nothing about the heritage of their ancestors and the spiritual heights they reached! No doubt, too, if the process of alienation from the church is accelerated, Orthodox congregations will be eliminated and will deplorably be diluted in the vast melting pot!"[62]

In the meantime, the Coptic church has responded to the fact that hundreds of thousands of her faithful members had left Egypt. Hundreds of Coptic churches have been founded in the Western world with the intent to provide a spiritual home for the emigrants. The Coptic Church has clearly decided to preserve at least her theological identity in the emigration, even if the ethnic identity may somehow evaporate over the years. In this respect Egyptians are different from emigrant Jews and Armenians. Their records show a very 'pure' ethnic identity in spite—or because of—severe persecution and rejection over centuries. Even in the nineteenth century many upper-class Egyptians married non-Egyptians, the Muslims Turkish women, and the Copts Europeans.

To retain a Coptic theological identity requires an unusually competent, well-trained and highly motivated clergy. It is questionable as to whether the contemporary Coptic Church is capable of facing today's challenging global responsibilities, and is in the position to muster the required manpower of parish priests, youth-workers, administrators, scholars, and bishops for this task. There is no doubt that the academic curricula of the theological schools in Egypt offer more than adequate information and guidance for local requirements, be they urban or rural. However, it is an altogether different matter for the Coptic parish clergy overseas. Just as Egyptian professionals (e.g., engineers, scientists, and businessmen) have chosen to attend graduate schools to equip themselves for a successful and enterprising life in the emigration, Coptic priests as parish-leaders require the technical 'know-how' that theological graduate schools provide. There, Coptic priests will be confronted with the whole spectrum of Western theology, sociology, pastoral psychology, church administration, and ecumenics. This is the kind of 'survival training' nowadays necessary for 'managing' the complexities of modern parish leadership. In fact, it is hoped that either the Coptic Church in Egypt, or the local parishes will invest in the priests—provided they stay for any length of time—for meaningful graduate studies. In addition to his role in the local ecumenical church council, the Coptic priest should participate in talk shows and attend the various local benevolent society meetings. In fact, as an 'exotic' clergyman he will attract many people who are eager to learn about the roots of the Christian faith, in a society in which the study of 'roots' happens to be in vogue. The chances for the Coptic Church in the emigration are limitless, and by the grace of God, He will send the right kind of leaders into his vineyard.

The Greek Orthodox Patriarchate of Alexandria and All Africa

Historical Note

As a result of the decisions of the fourth ecumenical Council of Chalcedon in 451, the non-Chalcedonian miaphysite pope Dioscorus, together with his archdeacon Timothy Aelurus, later Pope Timothy II Aelurus, were exiled to Gangra on the Black Sea. The Chalcedonian dyophysite, enjoying the political patronage of the emperor Marcian, was consecrated Proterios and became the first Chalcedonian pope of Alexandria (452–457). From the second half of the fifth century through to 536, the succession to the Alexandrian throne of St. Mark depended largely upon the support of the

Byzantine emperors. For the sake of religious and political unity they played a decisive role for maintaining the 'true' or Chalcedonian faith. After the assassination of Proterios, and while the non-Chalcedonian Pope Timothy II Aelurus, nicknamed the Cat, was still in exile in Chersonesus in the Crimea, the Chalcedonians succeeded in consecrating Timothy Salofaciolus of the Pachomian monastery as Canopus pope of Alexandria. Known for his ambiguous policies regarding throne and altar in both Constantinople and his Egyptian dioceses, he received the nickname 'Wobble Hat.' For the following fifty-seven years Timothy Wobble Hat was the last Chalcedonian pope of Alexandria.[63]

Following the papacy of the non-Chalcedonian Timothy III (518–536) in which they enjoyed the full support of the miaphysitic empress Theodora, wife of Justinian, the succession to the Alexandrian throne was permanently claimed and occupied by both Chalcedonian and non-Chalcedonian popes.

At the time of the conquest of Egypt by the Arabs in 641, the Chalcedonian pope Peter III (643–653), seeing that the country was definitely lost to the Byzatine empire, retired to Constantinople. On his death, the Greek Orthodox Patriarchate of Alexandria remained without a pope for some seventy years. The pontifical administrators resided in Constantinople most of the time.

In 727, Pope Cosmas I (727–787) returned to Alexandria and recovered for the Greek Orthodox Patriarchate the 'Great Church' *(Caesareum)* and the Angelion. From this time onwards, there has been a more or less regular succession of Greek Orthodox popes resident in Alexandria.

In addition to the Hellenic Greeks of the Greek Orthodox Church in Egypt, there exists a sizeable Greek Arabophone community. The Arabophone elements in the Greek Orthodox Church can be traced to the tenth century, when 'Abd al-Masih al-Halabi of Aleppo was consecrated as Patriarch Christoloulos of Alexandria. Whereas the Arabophone Greek Orthodox community in Syria increased over the centuries, it remained relatively small in Egypt. Following Greek independence from the Ottoman empire in 1932, many Greeks settled in Egypt and acquired a profound sense of ethnic nationalism. Due to tensions between the Hellenic Greeks and Arabophone Greeks, separate congregations and community centers were established in Cairo, Alexandria, Tanta, Mansura, and Port Said. Difficulties between the two communities occurred following the death of Pope Photios II in 1925, when the Arabophone notable and prince Michael Lutfallah pressed for the election of an Arabophone to the Greek Orthodox Patriarchate of Alexandria. The Arabophone demands for greater representation in church affairs were repeated during the ensuing patriarchates of Meletius II (1932), Nicholas V (1936), and Christophoros II (1939). In the Delta, Metropolitan Nicholas of Tanta serves a predominantly Arabophone Greek Orthodox community.

The Churches of the Greek Orthodox Church

The Greek Orthodox Patriarchate of Alexandria maintains the following churches in Egypt:

For the Patriarchate in Alexandria: St. Sabas the Hegumenon; the Annunciation of the Holy Virgin; St. Nicholas; the Dormition of the Holy Virgin; All-Archanges Prophet Elias; St. Paraskeve; St. Antonius the Great; the Unmercenary Saints *(Anargyroi)* in Abu Kir; St. Joseph of Arimathea and the Myrophores; St. George; St. Catherine; St. Alexander Nevsky (Russian); and St. Theodore and St. Mark.

For the Patriarchate in Cairo: St. Nicholas; Sts. Constantine and Helena; Archangel Michael; the Unmercenary Saints; St. Catherine, (Sinai *metochion*); St. Demetrios (Russian *metochion*) in Zeitun; the Dormition of the Holy Virgin, Old Cairo; St. George; and St. Panteleimon.

For the Metropolis of Memphis: The Holy Virgin, Heliopolis; St. Spyridon, Helwan; and the Presentation of the Holy Virgin in the Temple, Heliopolis.

For the Metropolis of Pelusium: The Transfiguration of Christ, Port Said; Sts. Athanasius and Cyril, Manasura; St. Nicholas, Damietta; and St. Spyridon, Kantara.

For the Metropolis of Hermopolis: St. George, St. Nicholas, and the Dormition of the Holy Virgin in Tanta; St. George in Kafr al Zayat; and St. Spyridon and the Presentation of Christ in the Temple (Hypapantes) in Shibin al-Kom.

For the Metropolis of Leontopolis: St. Menas and St. George, Ismailiya; St. Catherine, St. George, and St. Antonius, Port Tewfiq and Suez; and the Dormition of the Holy Virgin, Zaqaziq.

The Greek Orthodox Patriarchate of Alexandria maintains the following monasteries: in Alexandria: St. Sabas the Hegumenos; in Cairo: St. Nicholas; and in Old Cairo: St. George.

The Theological Differences between the Coptic Orthodox Church and the Greek Orthodox Church of Alexandria

The decisions of the fourth ecumenical council, held in 451 in Chalcedon, a suburb of Constantinople, were the reasons for the divisions of Alexandrian Christianity in the fifth century. As a response to the so-called 'Robber Council' of 449,[64] at which the Eutychian heresy was reinstated, some five hundred to six hundred Eastern bishops assembled in Chalcedon to lay the foundations for an orthodox canon of faith. Following tumultuous sessions, during which the proceedings of the Robber Council were annulled, Pope Dioscorus of Alexandria was deposed and banished. The council fathers accepted the Christological doctrine that "Christ had two natures, each perfect in itself and each distinct from the other, yet perfectly united in one person, who was at once both God and man." This statement, formally subscribed by the emperor Marcian, laid the foundation for Western and Byzantine Christology. The Eastern churches that adhered to the Christology of Chalcedon claimed the name 'orthodox.' These autocephalous churches included the Greek, Serbian, Russian, Rumanian, and Bulgarian churches, which considered the ecumenical patriarch of Constantinople as their *primus inter pares*. However, the ancient oriental churches (Armenians, Copts, Syrians, Ethiopians, and Malankar Syrian Indians) also claimed to be the true orthodox church, despite their rejection of the Christology of the Chalcedonian fathers. For fifteen hundred years, geographical isolation and lack of communication were some of the reasons for theological disagreements and frictions between these two communions.

Important opportunities occurred in the twentieth century. In ecumenical gatherings, like the Faith and Order Commission of the World Council of Churches, representatives of the Chalcedonian-dyophysitic churches met with those of the non-Chalcedonian-miaphysitic churches to begin joint efforts to overcome these centuries- old divisions. At the preparatory meetings at Aarhus (1964), Bristol (1967), Geneva (1970), and Addis Ababa (1971), agreement was reached with the acceptance of the Christological formula of Cyril of Alexandria "the one physis or hypotheses of God's word incarnate." Although the theologians of the two families of the fifth century had used different terminologies, their successors saw in the statement the same truth. Moreover, it was agreed that throughout the centuries of organic alienation the churches of both families had retained the apostolic faith and that dyophysites and miaphysites were truly orthodox. In fact, "ever since the fifth century, we have used different formulae to confess our common faith in the One Lord Jesus Christ, perfect God and perfect Man."[65] Indeed, mutual condemnations and anathematizations were not only improper but absolutely false. Regarding the acceptance of the seven ecumenical councils of the orthodox, a Coptic orthodox theologian declared in Bristol: "When the non-Chalcedonians do not receive juridically the later four Councils,[66] yet they receive the churches of the seven councils in communion, so they acknowledge indirectly the orthodoxy of the later four councils."[67]

In November 1987 the following hierarchs all gathered at the Coptic Orthodox Monastery of St. Bishoi to confirm again their Christological agreement: the Greek Orthodox Patriarch Parthenios III of Alexandria, the Coptic Orthodox Pope Shenuda III of Alexandria, the Greek Orthodox Patriarch Ignatios IV of Antioch, the Syrian Orthodox Patriach Ignatius Zakkas II was of Antioch, and the Armenian Catholicus Karekin II Sarkissian of Cilicia.

> We confirm our right understanding of the Person of Christ, Who is God from God, the only Son of the Father, who became truly man and has fully accepted our human nature, and made it one with His divinity without mingling, nor confusion, nor alteration. His divinity never departed from His humanity, even for a single moment nor the twinkling of an eye.

While full agreement was reached about the Christological issue that had separated the two orthodox families of dyophysites and miaphysites, several non-christological issues had yet to be solved. These pertained to the acceptance or non-acceptance of the seven ecumenical councils by the oriental orthodox churches, as well as the lifting of the mutual anthematizations and the liturgical acceptance of the saints of the other families. Most important, there still remained the problems of ecclesiastical jurisdiction. To this day, two popes claim to be the true and only successor of the Evangelist St. Mark. There is His Divine Beatitude Theodoros Pope and Patriarch of the great city of Alexandria and of all the Land of Egypt, of the City of our God, Jerusalem, of the Pentapolis, of Libya, Nubia, Ethiopia and all of Africa, Father of the Fathers and the thirteenth Apostle and Judge of the Universe.[68] He is the 124th successor of the Evangelist St. Mark.

For the Orthodox Copts, the head of the church is His Holiness Pope Shenuda III of Alexandria and Patriarch of the See of St. Mark. He is the 117th successor of the Evangelist St. Mark. This simple title was introduced by decree on May 10, 1959 at the consecration of Pope Cyril VI. The traditional title used to be: "Abba N. the most Holy Archbishop of the great city of Rakoti[69] and of Phostaton[70] of Babylon and the plains[71] of Egypt and Upper Egypt and the Pentapolis of Africa and the land of the Ethiopians and the Axumites and the Nobatai and the Makourians and the Bal an-Hmoou land."[72]

The Greek Orthodox Autocephalous Archdiocese of St. Catherine, Sinai

During the Decian (250) and Diocletian (303) persecutions, the Sinai mountains offered refuge for Egyptian Christians. The Spanish nun and pilgrim Egeria (390) provides the first detailed description of the churches on Mt. Moses, the Burning Bush (Exodus 3:1–12) and the Wadi Pharan. About 400, St. Nilus reports the martyrdom of forty Sinai monks. The first bishop of Pharan was the fifth-century Chalcedonian Macarius. Upon the request of the Sinai hermits, Emperor Justinian (527–565) built a monastery dedicated to the Holy Virgin at the foot of Mt. Moses. In the sixth century, monks of Sinai (Anastasius and Gregory I) were elected as patriarchs of Antioch. In the seventh century Pope Gregory I of Rome provided the Sinaites with help for a hospice. In the tenth century the traditions of the Alexandrian virgin-martyr St. Catherine reached the Sinaites (Simeone Metaphrastes). From the twelfth to fifteenth centuries the monks of St. Catherine collected alms for their monastery in exchange for their patron's relics. During the Latin kingdom of Jerusalem (1099–1187), the Greek Orthodox archbishop of Sinai was suffragen of the Latin archbishop of Petra. Throughout the Middle Ages, the Orthodox patriarchs of Alexandria and Jerusalem disputed the jurisdiction of the arch-episcopal See of Sinai. In the thirteenth century, Pope Honorius III of Rome confirmed the protection of the Roman Catholic Church against other hierarchs. From the sixteenth to eighteenth centuries, the Monastery of St. Catherine was repeatedly abandoned.

Following the jurisdictional disputes between 1575 and 1782 the archdiocese of St. Catherine was declared autocephalous, and confirmed by the Greek Orthodox Synod of Constantinople 1782. In 1844, 1853, and

1859, Konstantin von Tischendorf acquired the fourth-century *Codex Sinaiticus* for Friedrich August, King of Saxony, and Czar Alexander II of Russia. In 1892, Agnes Smith Lewis discovered the fourth-century Codex Syriacus, a palimpsest of a second-century version of the New Testament.

On Saturday, February 26, 2000, Pope John Paul II was the first Roman pontiff to visit the Monastery of St. Catherine and venerate the site of the Burning Bush.

The Greek Orthodox Archbishops of Sinai were: 1759 Cyril II of Crete; 1804 Constantine of Constantinople; 1859 Cyril III; 1867 Callistratos; 1885 Porphyrios I of Zakinthos; 1904 Porphyrios II of Limnos; 1926 Porphyrios III of Euboia; 1969 Gregorios II of Smyrna; and 1973 Damianos.

The Armenian Orthodox Church in Egypt

Historical Note

Armenians have held important administrative positions in Egypt ever since the days of the Byzantine rule in Egypt, as well as in the other parts of the Byzantine Empire. Thus, during the reign of the Emperor Justinian (527–565), an Armenian General, Nerseh Pasentzi, is reported to have conquered parts of Africa. In 545, the Emperor sent an army to Libya, which was composed largely of Armenian soldiers, under the leadership of Ardavans Arshagouni, who was accompanied by Vahan, his brother, Krikor, his nephew, and Arshadir, his relative. Later the Emperor Justinian raised Ardavane to the rank of Governor of Libya and Duke of Africa. During this period, many Armenians came to Egypt, where subsequently they built many churches. In 553 when the Emperor persecuted the Armenian Church in Jerusalem, and forced them to accept the Chalcedonian Creed, a considerable number left Jerusalem and settled in Egypt.

The Arab, ‘Amr ibn al-‘As, when he conquered Egypt in 641, built the city of Fustat near the site of ancient Babylon. He was assisted by his friend Vartan al-Rumi in this work. After ‘Amr's death, Vartan was appointed chief tax collector.

During the Fatimid period, the Armenian community in Egypt spread from one part of the country to the other, and many Armenian churches were built throughout the Nile Valley. In Cairo, there was a gate called Bab al-Arman. According to Abu Makarim and al-Maqrizi, the Armenians had thirty-five churches and monasteries in Egypt. There was, for example, the Church of the Holy Virgin in the Harat Zuwaila. This church formerly belonged to the

Melkites. In 1076, however, Badr al-Gamali the powerful head of the Fatimid Government, who was Armenian by origin, gave it to the Armenians on the occasion of the visit of Gregory II, the Catholicus of Armenia, to Egypt.

The Church of St. George of Dair al-Khandaq belonged to the Copts. It was, however, in ruins when, about 1084, on the demand of the Archbishop Gregory, Badr al-Gamali gave it to the Armenians, who rebuilt it. In 1168, the Church of St. James at al-Basatin was rebuilt. The Church of St. George at Dura, near al-Basatin, which belonged to the Copts, was given to the Armenians, when they increased in numbers. The Armenians demolished this church, and built a larger structure with a belfry and high walls around it. The Church of St. Gregory was near the Church of St. George at Dura. In 1164 it was in the possession of the Armenians, though by 1204 the Copts had acquired it. The Church of St. George at Giza was also a large and important one, in which the Armenians owned property. Near Girga, the Armenians owned the Church of St. George and in al-Qas'a, north of Asyut, they owned a monastery and two churches. Armenian monks also inhabited the White Monastery near Sohag.

During the rule of the Ayyubids (1171–1250), the Armenians were persecuted, because of their alliance to the Fatimids, and the Armenian army was disbanded by the Sultan Salah al-Din. During this period, several Armenian churches were acquired by the Copts, though some of them were returned to the Armenians later.

During the Mamluk period (1250–1517), Armenian influence declined, and many churches were destroyed in 1322, and again in 1389. By 1517, for example, there were no Armenians in Alexandria, though Armenians and Turks lived in the Khan al-Khalili, where they worked as goldsmiths and jewelers.

The rule of Muhammad 'Ali was more favorable to Armenians. He surrounded himself with many, some of them serving as members of the Egyptian Cabinet, and we hear of men like Boghos Bey Yousoufian, Garabed Noubrian, Artin Bey Cherakian, Arisdages Altoune Duri, Khosrov Cherakian, and Arakel Bey Noubar. After the death of Muhammad 'Ali, they continued to serve in the Egyptian Government, the most prominent of whom were Yousuf Artin Bey, Tito Pasha Hakikian, Yeghiazar Amira, Artin Bey Cherakian, and Stephen Bey Demirdhian. Nubar Pasha served from 1866 to 1888 in the Ministry of Foreign Affairs, and held the office of prime minister twice.

Some of the more outstanding Armenian prelates in Egypt were the following archbishops: Gabriel (1830–1867), Meguerditch (1864–1866), Mesrob (1867–1879), Mattaus (1886–1890), Hagop (1897–1899), Hovsep (1900–1904), Meguerditch (1905–1912), and Jorghom (1914–1931).

Since 1950, the size of the Armenian community has declined from some forty thousand to about fifteen thousand, owing to large-scale emigration, mostly to the Soviet Union. They have two daily newspapers and three weekly magazines. One of the first printing presses in Egypt was established in 1865 by Abraham Mouradian, who in cooperation with Bishop Meguerditch Kefsizian, published a newspaper called *Armaveni*. Later on, Father Ghevont Papzian, Vahan Mamourian, and Andon Reshdouni published the weekly newspaper *Neghos*.

The Churches of the Armenian Diocese

The Armenian Churches in Egypt belong to the Patriarchate of Echmiadzin. The head of the Armenian Church in Egypt is an Archbishop, who is elected by the combined vote of the twenty-four members of the Legislative Council in Cairo, and a corresponding Legislative Council in Alexandria.

The Armenian Orthodox Cathedral at Ramses Street, Cairo, is dedicated to St. Gregory the Illuminator. The Armenian Orthodox Church in Alexandria is dedicated to Sts. Peter and Paul.

The Syrian Orthodox Church in Egypt

The relationship of the Syrian Orthodox (Jacobite) Church to the Egyptian Church is for the most part one of cordiality and friendship. The practice of sending synodical letters from the Patriarch of Alexandria to the Patriarch of Antioch is first mentioned in the middle of the third century, when Dionysius the Wise, fourteenth Patriarch of Alexandria (247–264), sent a letter to Fabius, Patriarch of Antioch, reporting on the martyrs who suffered in Alexandria under the terror of Decius. The relationship between the Sees increased in cordiality following the acceptance of the miaphysite doctrines by the Syrian Christians. True, for a hundred years after the Council of Chalcedon, there had been a constant contention between the dyophysites and the miaphysites, and the Patriarch of Antioch vacillated between the two doctrines. Severus was the best known miaphysite patriarch and occupied the See from 512–518. In the end he was compelled to seek refuge in Alexandria. The most influential patriarch in the formation of the Miaphysite See of Antioch was was Jacob Baradaeus. He was consecrated in secret by Theodosius I, Patriarch of Alexandria, in 536. He was given a roving commission to consecrate and organize a miaphysite hierarchy. From the sixth century onwards, one of the duties of the newly consecrated patriarchs of Alexandria and Antioch was to send synodical messages to each other, thus reaffirming their doctrinal allegiance. Despite the attempt made by Damian, the thirty-fifth Patriarch of Alexandria (569–605), to establish Alexandria as a kind of 'miaphysite papacy,' the dream was never realized. On the contrary, the theological leadership within miaphysitism passed at a very early date into the hands of the Antiochenes.

Apart from a small number of Syrians who came to Egypt in the third and fourth centuries, a Syrian colony of some importance emerged in the seventh century in and around Alexandria, and Syrian monks engaged in scholarly pursuits at the Ennaton. Among them was Thomas of Harkel, who revised the Syriac version of the Bible from Greek manuscripts. In 616, we even hear of a divine service at the Ennaton, in which both the Alexandrian and the Antiochene patriarchs participated.

The Monastery of the Syrians in the Wadi al-Natrun was founded in the sixth century as a consequence of the Gaianite heresy. It was the duplicate, or Theotokos monastery of the Monastery of St. Bishoi, to which the Orthodox monks withdrew. The name Theotokos, or Mother of God monastery, was derived from the importance with which the Orthodox monks regarded the doctrine of the Incarnation. The teachings of the Gaianites were considered by their opponents as a Docetist heresy, which denying the doctrine of the Incarnation, lowered the status of the Holy Virgin Mary. To emphasize their Orthodoxy, they retained the name of the Patron Saint and added to it the title of the Theotokos. Thus the Monastery of the Syrians was known as the Theotokos Monastery of St. Bishoi.

The first Syrian monks to be associated with the monastery arrived in the Wadi al-Natrun at the beginning of the ninth century. They were Matthew and Abraham of Tekrit, and there is good reason to believe that they settled in the Western desert about the time of the fifth sack of the desert monasteries.

By the eleventh century, according to the census taken by Mawhub, the Syrian monastery rated as the third largest community in the Wadi al-Natrun. With its sixty monks, it was as large as the Monastery of St. Bishoi and the Monastery of the Romans together.

In the middle of the fourteenth century, the monastery suffered a most serious setback, for at this time the Black Death swept over Egypt and took a terrible toll of the Wadi al-Natrun monks. A note in a Syriac manuscript states that a visitor to the Monastery of the Syrians found but a single monk.

By the end of the fifteenth century, the monastery seems to have recuperated, for when Ignatius XI, Patriarch of Antioch, visited, the monastery was inhabited by Syrian monks. In 1516, there was a total of forty-three monks, of whom eighteen were Syrians and twenty-five Egyptians. The German Lutheran missionary Peter Heyling (1634) provided the last reference to Syrian monks in the monasteries of the Wadi al-Natrun.

The Syrian Orthodox (Jacobite) community in Cairo is very small, numbering no more than two hundred families.

The Catholic Church in Egypt

The Beginnings of the Roman Catholic Mission in Egypt

St. Francis of Assisi

Following the military and political disasters of the first four crusades between 1096 and 1204, a fifth crusade (1218–1221) was formed during the pontificate of Innocent III. Its purpose was the recovery of Jerusalem, where peace and tranquility had prevailed during the forty years since the loss of the city in 1187. In the course of the fourth Lateran Council in 1215 the pope proclaimed a crusade for 1217, and Egypt was selected as the first goal of the principle attack. When Pope Innocent III died in 1216, everything was ready for the crusade by a siege of Damietta, on the eastern branch of the Nile, a few miles above its mouth, was their first goal, and was laid to siege. The original leader of the crusade was John of Brienne, King of Jerusalem, but after the end of 1218, the cardinal legate Pelagius claimed the command. In spite of the dissensions between the cardinal and the king, and the various offers made by Sultan al-Malik al-Kamil Muhammad, the crusaders finally carried the siege to a successful conclusion at the end of 1219. Though the capture of Damietta was a military success, nothing followed to maintain the advantage.

At the age of twenty-four, Francis of Assisi experienced a life-determining episode. Having had a special fear and horror of lepers, one day he passed a leper and in an act of self-conquest he gave him not only money but also kissed his hand. For the following three years he lived in poverty, ministering to outcasts and lepers, until one day, while attending the little ruined chapel of St. Mary of the Angels, known as the Portiuncula, he accepted the words of the Gospel: "Preach as you go, saying 'The Kingdom of heaven is at hand.' Heal the sick, raise the dead, cleanse lepers, cast out demons. You received without pay, give without pay. Take no gold, nor silver, nor copper in your belts, no bag for your journey, nor two tunics, nor sandals, nor staff, for the laborer deserves his food" (Matthew 10: 7–10). After twelve disciples had joined him, he obtained sanction from Pope Innocent III to preach and serve the poor.

Francis had first set out for the Holy Land in 1212, but was shipwrecked and had to return. Two years later he preached to the Muslims in Spain, but without success and he returned to Umbria. On May 26, 1219, the Founder of the Franciscan order summoned his second General Chapter. The mission to the East was led by Brother Elias, and that to Spain by Brother Bernard. Brother Giles and some others were appointed to go to Tunis. Francis chose twelve companions to take with him to Egypt. With Pietro of Cattani as his escort, he reached Ancona, whence a band of crusaders was about to set sail for Egypt. After his arrival in Damietta, Francis expected to have an opportunity to meet the Ayyubid Sultan al-Kamil Muhammad (1218–1238). He thought that if he could win him to the Christian faith it would mean a victory for Christ throughout the empire of his uncle Salah al-Din (1169–1193).

At the beginning of September 1219 a truce was signed between the two belligerents who were both exhausted. This armistice was the signal for Francis to launch his missionary offensive. Furnished with necessary papers, he reached the tent of the Sultan al-Kamil. It was well known that the sultan was favourably disposed toward his Christian subjects. According to historians, Francis remained for nearly a month at the Sultan's court, preaching daily with the same zeal, but also with the same lack of success. Upon the renewal of hostilities, Francis had to leave the camp.

Following the fall of Damietta on November 5, 1219, Francis proceeded to the Holy Land where he remained until March 1221 when he was recalled to Italy.

From a Mission to Muslims to a Mission the Schismatics

The purpose of the first Roman Catholic missions to the East was to preach the Gospel of Jesus Christ to Muslims, as in the case of St. Francis and the early Franciscans. Realizing, however, their lack of success to convert the followers of Muhammad to be believers in Jesus Christ, the Christian missionaries changed their strategy. By the fifteenth century, the Roman

Catholic Church turned to the 'schismatic' Oriental Orthodox Christians to convince them to accept 'the true faith,' as proclaimed by the pope of Rome.

The Council of Ferrara and Florence

In order to bridge the gap between the church of Rome and the Orthodox churches of the East, and to win back the power and prestige which the papacy had lost over the years, Pope Eugenius IV (1431–1447) called an ecumenical council in Ferrara for the spring of 1438. The union with the orthodox churches of the East was to reinstate the papacy to its previous position, at least in the eyes of Europe. The pope's ambition was to appear as the one and only leader of Christendom.

After the theological discussions with the orthodox Greeks in Ferrara, the council moved in the summer of 1438 to Florence. The main theological issues focused on the use of leavened or unleavened bread in the Eucharist, the question of purgatory, and the thorny problem of the *filioque* (the discussion whether the Holy Spirit proceeds from the Father only or from the Father and the Son), and, of course, the principle consideration of the 1439 teaching of the papal supremacy. Whereas some agreement was reached, the main issues remained unsolved, and remain so today!

Following a formal adjournment, the Coptic and the Ethiopian representatives arrived at the scene. The Coptic Pope John XI (1427–1452) had sent Yuhannes, the abbot of the Red Sea Monastery of St. Antony and Nicodemus, and the prior of the Ethiopian Monastery in Jerusalem, to represent their churches at the council. For the Roman Catholics the Orthodox Copts and Ethiopians were known as Jacobites, after the sixth century Syrian miaphysitic preacher and theologian Jacob Baradaeus. On February 4, 1442 Pope Eugenius IV finally published the *Decretum pro Jacobitis*, a summary of controversial theological issues, that separated the Roman Catholic church from the Oriental orthodox churches. The desired union remained in abeyance. In spite of this failure, the Roman Catholic popes continued their policy to unite the Copts with the See of Rome.

The Age of Papal Diplomacy

In September 1540, St. Ignatius of Loyola founded the society of Jesus, an order that was approved by Pope Paul III in his famous *Bull Regimini Militantis Eclesiea*, for the propagation of the Roman Catholic faith throughout the world. Twenty years later, Pope Pius IV (1559–1569) sent two Jesuit missionaries to Egypt to bring about the union of the Coptic Church with the See of Rome. They were Father Giambattista Eliano, a Jewish convert, and Father Christoforo Rodriguez. They were received by the Coptic Pope Gabriel VII (1525–1568), but no results of their meeting were recorded. Father Francois Sasso, another Jesuit missionary with a letter from Pope Gregory XIII (1572–1585) approached the Coptic Pope John XIV (1573–1589). Father François Sasso even attended the holy synod of the Coptic Church on February 1, 1584. The results of this mission remained ambiguous and contested.

A few years later, the Coptic Pope Gabriel VIII (1585–1602) issued a statement according to which he recognized the supremacy of the Roman pontiff. This document was written in the small Upper Egyptian Monastery of St. Victor in Abnub, on the east bank of the Nile opposite Asyut in January 1590. This confession was addressed to Pope Sixtus V (1585–1590) and contained the willingness of the Coptic pope to unite with the Roman Catholic Church. Father Ghobrial al-Muharraqi, Archdeacon Barsum of the Cathedral of St. Mark in Alexandria, and Father Ghobrial, a monk of the Monastery of the Holy Virgin at Gebel al-Tair submitted this document in Rome.

On January 15, 1595 Pope Clement VIII (1592–1602), in the presence of twenty-four cardinals, received the Coptic delegation of Pope Gabriel VIII. In his name they offered the confession of faith, namely the formula set forth by Pope Gregory XIII around ten years earlier, professing full and absolute obedience to the pope of Rome. Two years later, on June 28, 1597, the Coptic delegation of Gabriel VIII returned to Rome with the ratified documents of reunion and were granted an audience with Pope Clement VIII. However, since these new documents did not grant sufficient autonomy to the Coptic Church and demanded the promise of full and absolute obedience to the pope of Rome, this effort remained practically ineffective.

The Capuchin Missionary Efforts in the Coptic Monasteries

Sultan Murad IV ruled Egypt from 1623–1640 through eight pashas or walis. The pontifical throne of St. Mark was occupied by Yuhannis XV (1619–1629), formerly a monk of the Monastery of St. Antony. During his term of office new and additional taxes were imposed upon the Copts, known as *al-gawali*. In addition, they were subjected to other forms of harassments. For example, they were forbidden to walk on the right side of the street, to ride horses, or to wear any color other than black.

In Rome, a committee of cardinals under the name of the *Congregatio de Propaganda Fide* was appointed in 1622 to give unity and solidity to the missionary work of the Roman Catholic Church. The scheme originated with Pope Gregory XIII, but became effective with a bull of Gregory XV (1621–1623). The missionary work in Egypt, and particularly the efforts of reuniting the schismatic Copts with the See of Rome, was entrusted to the Capuchins from 1619. Their work in Egypt fell into the long reign of the Barberini Pope Urban VIII (1623–1644). Whereas the Catholic revival in central Europe was somewhat paralyzed by the Thirty Years War, it did bear some fruit in overseas territories. It was Pope Urban VIII, who created the Propaganda College and the famous Propaganda Press for the spread of the Gospel.

The Capuchins at the Monastery of St. Antony

There were several factors that led the Capuchin missionaries to concentrate their efforts upon the Coptic monks of the Monastery of St. Antony. There was a significant Ethiopian community that resided with the Coptic monks in this monastery. According to the Dominican scholar J. M. Wansleben, these Ethiopians used to have a monastery within the monastery, which at the time of his visit in 1672, however, was in ruins.

The head of the Ethiopian Church, the Abuna, was traditionally a Coptic monk from one of the Egyptian monasteries and was consecrated by the Coptic pope. Contacts with the monks of the Monastery of St. Antony were, therefore, highly advantageous for the conversion of the Ethiopian Church, especially since the sixteenth-century Jesuit mission to Ethiopia had failed to achieve its goal. However, Ethiopia was not to be abandoned so far as the Roman Catholic Church was concerned.

In addition to the 'Ethiopian connection,' it was well known that the Monastery of St. Antony had supplied the See of St. Mark with the ninety-ninth successor of the Evangelist, Pope Yuhannis XV (1619–1629). During the seventeenth century, the Monastery of St. Antony became the most important Coptic monastery. Between the seventeenth and nineteenth centuries, ten out of twelve popes were monks from this monastery. Also the properties of the Holy Land in general, and in Jerusalem in particular, were served by monks from St. Antony's. In 1623 Pope Urban VIII sent Capuchin missionaries to Egypt, headed by Father Paolo di Lodi to work among the

Copts. In the course of this mission, one Capuchin friar went to the Monastery of St. Antony in 1626. His visit to the monastery is well documented by several dated graffiti in the churches of St. Antony and St. Mark. On the western wall of the narthex of the Church of St. Antony he wrote in large black letters: "*Fr B...ardus ferulensis siculus sub die X Ianuary 1626*" (Brother Bernardus of Feroleto (or Ferulensis) of Sicily on January 10, 1626). On the upper beam of the wooden choir-screen of the Church of St. Anthony the same friar added the following text: "*Frater Bernardus a Ferula Siculus de Observatia*" (Brother Bernardus of Feroleto of Sicily belonging to the Observantia).

The Church of St. Mark lies in the extensive palm grove and fruit-and-vegetable garden of the monastery. Apparently, this church was allotted by the Copts to the Capuchin fathers who had established themselves in the monastery during the second quarter of the seventeenth century. Until a few years ago, the Terra Santa Cross above the entrance to the Church of St. Mark used to bear witness to this association. On the northern wall of this church, the reliquary of the saint (this is not the Evangelist Mark, but a monk of the monastery, to whom this church is dedicated) is separated from the nave by a simple wooden screen. Upon the upper beam of the screen there is the following text in black paint or ink: "ubi celebra (vi) quadraginta diebus X ultra" (Where I have celebrated forty days and more). On the wooden screen separating the northern from the central haikal, there are two lines of the text: "*Fr. Bernardus Trigilius Ferulensis Ordinis Minorum de observantia Provinciae Siculae*" (Brother Bernardus Trigilius of Fereleto of the Friars Minor of the Observantia of the Province of Sicily). Lower line: "*H(a)ec aedes est Fr(at)ris Bernardi Ferulensis Siculi*" (This room belongs to Brother Bernardus of Fereleto of Sicily).

Moreover, in the cave of St. Antony situated 680 meters above sea level and 276 meters above the Monastery of St. Antony, the date 1626 is written in the same hand on the upper south wall. Unfortunately, with the rapid increase of pilgrims and visitors to the desert monasteries many of these medieval graffiti are gradually disappearing.

By 1630, the Capuchins had established themselves in the Monastery of St. Antony. Here they learned Arabic in preparation for their missionary work among the Arabic-speaking Copts. A letter written by Father Andrea d'Arco to the *Propaganda* in Rome, dated February 23, 1639, suggests that the *Propaganda* pay the Coptic monks of the Monastery of St. Antony the amount of forty *scudi* annually, so that two or three Capuchins could reside there for the purpose of studying the Arabic language. For the Capuchin missionaries there was no better way to acquaint themselves with the theology, piety, and language than to enter a Coptic monastery. A letter written by Father Antonius de Virgoletta to the *Propaganda* on April 18, 1639 requests the authorities to send new missionaries to the Monasteries of St. Macarius in the Wadi al-Natrun and St. Antony so that they could learn Arabic within seven or eight months, rather than in seven years elsewhere.

The result of this missionary strategy is evident from the reports which were sent from Egypt to the ecclesiastical authorities in Europe. Father Sylvester of St. Aignain reported in 1651 that even the patriarch (Matthew III, 1634–1649) permitted him to preach in the Coptic churches, and Father Johannes Baptista of St. Aignam sent a detailed account of the Capuchin mission to the French minister Jean Baptiste Colbert. In this report he mentioned, that after 1630 the fathers often preached in the churches of the Copts, that they absolved many Copts, including priests and monks. Apparently, this was done in spite of the prohibition of the *Sacra Congregatio de Propaganda Fide*, which prohibited the *Communicatio in sacris cum dissentibus* (the joint participation of the sacraments with schismatics) of March 21, 1627.

The leading spirit among the Capuchin missionaries was undoubtedly Father Agathangelus, who, together with Father Cassien of Nantes visited all the Coptic monasteries. He stayed for a period of four months at the Monastery of St. Antony conducting doctrinal discussions and offering spiritual conferences. Two out of fifteen monks were even reconciled with the Church of Rome.

The Capuchins at the Monastery of St. Macarius

The Monastery of St. Macarius is situated in the historic Desert of Scetis, Wadi al-Natrun, between Cairo and Alexandria. It was the most important Coptic monastery in the Middle Ages. In the eleventh century, there were still seven active monasteries in the Wadi al-Natrun with 737 monks, four hundred of whom inhabited the Monastery of St. Macarius. Ever since the days of the Emperor Justinian (sixth century), the Monastery of St. Macarius had served on and off as the residence of the Coptic popes. Moreover, one of the functions of the Coptic popes has always been the consecration of the Holy Myron in the Monastery of St. Macarius. In addition, the monks used to play an important role in the selection of the Coptic leadership.

The fact that the monastery had been home to one of the most significant Coptic libraries since the Middle Ages was undoubtedly one reason that attracted the missionaries to the desert monastery. These treasures, no doubt, were partly due to the grant that the Emperor Zeno (474–491) had bestowed upon the monastery.

The first study and description of the Coptic monasteries, largely focusing on their libraries, was presented by the Capuchin father Cassien of Nantes to French archeologist and collector Nicholas C.F. de Peiresc in the *Correspondence de Peiresc avec plusieurs missionaries et religieux de l'ordre des Capucins 1631–1637*. In his desire to obtain as many volumes as possible, Peiresc used the services of the Capuchin missionaries. Father Aegidius Lochiensis had reported to Peiresc the variety of rare books extant in in the numerous convents and monasteries. At St. Macarius he saw eight thousand manuscripts! Father Agathangelus of Vendôme, who was sent to Egypt in pursuit of these treasures, wrote to Peiresc from Cairo in 1634 informing him that he was on the point of securing a manuscript of the Psalms from the monks of the Monastery of St. Macarius. The most remarkable manuscript obtained by Father Agathangelus was the famous *Codex Barberianus Orientalis*, a polyglot psalter written in five columns, in Ethiopic, Syriac, Coptic, Arabic, and Armenian. This manuscript was sent to Peiresc, but was captured on the way by pirates and taken to Tripoli, where it was bought back. Subsequently, it was lost again, but rediscovered in 1637 and bought for Cardinal F. Barberini by John Paul Lascarius.

The graffiti in the Chapel of St. Michael in the keep *(qasr)* is proof that the monastery was visited frequently in the middle of the seventeenth century. The names and initials of three seventeenth-century visitors are scratched on the plaster of the north wall: CLAUD DURAND 1640; M. M. 1640; and ANTHOINE BA . . . 1644. It is very likely that during this period the monastery served as a training school for the Capuchin missionaries in the same manner as the Monastery of St. Antony. A letter sent on April 18, 1639 by Father Anthonius de Virgoletta to the *Propaganda* states among other things that missionaries were to be sent to the Monastery of St. Macarius for the purpose of studying the Arabic language. It is quite possible that this Father Anthonius is the ANTHOINE BA who left his graffito on the wall of the chapel in 1644. In or around 1638, Father Franciscus of Como, who worked with Father Marcus of Lucca, for the union of the Copts with the Church of Rome stayed at the monastery. Father Franciscus became a teacher of Arabic in Jerusalem, and later the custodian of the Terra Santa in the Holy City.

Toward a Coptic Catholic Church

From the middle of the fifteenth century, the Roman Catholic Church was increasingly engaged in healing the theological schisms that had divided Christendom. The Roman Catholic hierarchy had just recovered from its contests with the fifteenth-century reforming councils of Pisa (1409), Constance (1415), and Basel (1431). Pope Eugenius IV had successfully ignored his suspension by the last of these three councils in 1438. By calling an ecumenical council in 1438 to assemble in Ferrara and later in Florence, he hoped to strengthen his position as leader of the universal church, while at the same time also healing the divisions that had separated the churches ever since the middle of the fifth century. Following the theologically and structurally ineffective outcome of the council of Ferrara and Florence, several attempts were made in Egypt during the Coptic pontificate of John XIV (1571–1586) to have the Coptic Church join the Roman Catholic Church, but these endeavors also failed.

An unexpected political and economic development occurred during the first few years of the eighteenth century that led to a significant expansion of the Catholic missionary enterprises especially in Upper Egypt. The so-called 'foreign capitulation system' was the result of several treaties between the Sublime Porte and various European countries which permitted foreigners in Egypt to live, trade, and purchase property without paying taxes. Moreover, foreigners were not subject to local laws, nor were they to be tried by Egyptian courts.

About a hundred years before, the Franciscan fathers had established their first houses in Alexandria and Cairo. In 1682 they had decided to divide their responsibilities. The Franciscans of the Custody of the Holy Land were to work in Cairo and Lower Egypt, while the Upper Egyptian Mission was to concentrate on the regions south of Cairo. In Upper Egypt, Catholic priests opened schools for boys, thereby laying foundations for Coptic Catholic parishes.

Realizing the need for some form of spiritual leadership, Pope Benedict XIV (1740–1758) consecrated the first Coptic Catholic bishop in 1741 by the name of Athanasius. However, neither he nor his two successors ever resided in Egypt. As apostolic vicars for Egypt they lived in Jerusalem. It was at this time that Rufa'il al-Tukhi converted to Catholicism. He fled to Rome, where he spent the years 1736–1749 editing the Coptic-Arabic Euchologion, as well as other liturgical books.

In 1731, there were nine Coptic Catholic parishes in Upper Egypt. As a result of the successful Upper Egyptian Franciscan Mission in 1738, twenty-four Coptic orthodox notables procured a decree from the Egyptian government which prohibited orthodox Copts from converting to Catholicism. In 1794, an agreement was reached that prohibited mixed marriages between orthodox and Catholic Copts. Throughout the eighteenth century, Roman Catholics enjoyed the protection of Venice. For that matter, their Cairo mission used the facilities of the Venetian embassy on Bendaka Street, Muski. Later, the Austrians accepted the protection of the Roman Catholic missionaries. This included both political as well as financial support. Until the establishment of the Mixed Courts in 1876, the Catholic Copts enjoyed the legal privileges of the Austrians according to the laws of the foreign capitulations.

Toward the end of the eighteenth century, Pope Pius VI (1775–1799) sent a delegation under Father Bartholomew to the Coptic Pope Yuannis XVIII (1769–1796) stressing the advantages for the church and his people if they acknowledged the sovereignty of the Pope of Rome. The pope listened to the advances by the Catholic theologians. Then he asked his most competent and learned theologian to write a reply. Abba Yusab ibn l'Abahh, Bishop of Girga and Akhmim (1735–1826), set himself to the task and expounded the orthodox doctrines of the doctors and fathers of the Church of St. Mark. This reply was sent to Pope Pius VI and for a few years, at least, the Roman pontiffs suspended their efforts to win the Coptic Church. In the Church of the Apostles in the Red Sea Monastery of St. Antony reposes the uncorrupted body of this unusual theologian. He was known not only for his theological eloquence but also for his sanctity. He is commemorated on January 24.

During the reign of Muhammad 'Ali (1805–1848) and the pontificate of Peter VII al-Gawli (1809–1852) a way for an independent Coptic Catholic Church was finally cleared, though not by theological process but rather by political skill and ingenuity. The French consul-general, realizing the amiability of Muhammad 'Ali toward France, suggested to the Khedive that he use his authority to sway the Coptic hierarchy, the pope, and the important bishops to accept the teachings of the Roman Catholic Church and to join the See of Rome. The Khedive called his secretary Mu'allim Ghali, his brother Francis, and his son Basilius to inform them of the French proposal. The Coptic notables realized that neither Pope Peter VII, nor any significant number of the bishops or notables, would even consider accepting such a proposition. However, for the sake of making the Khedive appear successful in the eyes of his French allies, the three Ghalis, their families, dependents, servants, and acquaintances joined the Roman Catholic Church. This happened in January 1822. Only six months later, on July 1, 1822, Mu'allim Ghali was assassinated by one of Muhammad 'Ali's own men. His brother Francis had forged a document in the Khedive's name with his signature requesting the the pope in Rome consecrate a friend of his as Archbishop of Memphis. Moreover, he was to coerce the Copts to submit to the See of Rome. Enfuriated by this act, Muhammad 'Ali ordered Ghali's assassination in accordance with the oriental practice that the head of the family is responsible for the actions of its members. This acceptance of the teachings of the Roman Catholic Church on the part of Mu'allim Ghali, his family, and followers formed the beginning of the Coptic Catholic Church.

The Coptic Catholic Patriarchate of Alexandria

On August 1, 1824, Pope Leo XII (1823–1829) consecrated Abraham Khashur, a young Coptic alumnus of the Propaganda College in Rome, as bishop for the Catholic Copts. In the bull *Patrus Apostolorum Princeps* of August 15, 1824, Leo XII established the Coptic Catholic Patriarchate of Alexandria. However, this patriarchate remained only on paper and the Coptic Catholics were administered and ruled by apostolic vicars. In 1854 Pope Pius IX (1846–1878) appointed Athanasius Khusam as administrator of the Catholic Copts. In September 1895, Catholic Copts, headed by the apostolic vicar Cyril Maqar, petitioned Pope Leo XIII (1873–1905) to form a Coptic Catholic Patriarchate of Alexandria and to erect it for all Copts. This request was fulfilled in the apostolic letter *Christi Domini* of November 27, 1895. Cyril Maqar was appointed apostolic administrator of the patriarchate. In his apostolic letter, Leo XIII had stated that "this Catholic patriarchate was the only one which legitimately rules the church founded by St. Mark, the only heir of all the memories faithfully handed down from the pristine and glorious times of the Patriarchate of Alexandria." Therefore, from a juridical Roman Catholic point of view, the orthodox Patriarchate of Alexandria was a legal fiction which canonically did not even exist.

Instead of quietly acting within this jurisdiction of Catholic Copts, the new apostolic vicar began to issue encyclicals addressed to members of orthodox congregations and their priests, inviting them to offer allegiance to the pope of Rome. The Coptic liturgy was fully adopted with the necessary intercessions for the pope in Rome. This meant that many Copts could not distinguish the differences in the orders of service. Pope Cyril V (1874–1927) replied to these Catholic missionary efforts with a long and forceful encyclical, which was read by all orthodox bishops and priests throughout Upper and Lower Egypt. Coptic priests and theologians warned their parishioners of the dangers of falling into the hands of the Catholics. A decisive role in this ensuing controversy was played by the Hegoumenos Filuthaus Ibrahim (1837–1904). As priest at the Patriarchal Cathedral he became well known for his homiletical abilities. In his polemics Filuthaus Ibrahim attacked the Catholic Church, especially in his *The Orthodox Evidence against Roman Talk*, in which he discussed the spiritual equality of the apostles, and consequently that of the patriarchs.

A general synod of the Coptic Catholic Church in 1898 decided upon major Latinizing changes in the liturgical and devotional life of the Church. Reflecting the nineteenth-century piety of the European missionaries, purely Roman Catholic practices such as the veneration of the Sacred Heart, Corpus Christi, the Immaculate Conception, and the devotion to St. Joseph were introduced. The procession of the Holy Spirit from the Father and the Son, one of the Christological stumbling blocks in the ecumenical debates, was accepted. The Coptic Catholic Church was dedicated to the Sacred Heart of Jesus, a cult peculiar to the modern Roman Catholic Church, based upon the visions of the French nun St. Marguerita Marie Alocoque (1647–1690). In 1856 Pope Pius IX had introduced this feast into the general calendar of the Roman Catholic Church, fixing the Friday after the Octave of Corpus Christi for its celebration. The institution of the medieval feast of Corpus Christi is due to the visions of St. Juliana, prioress of Mt. Cornillon, Liège (1222–1258), regarding the veneration of the Blessed Sacrament. In 1264 Pope Urban IV ordered the general observation of this feast. The doctrine of the Immaculate Conception was defined by Pope Pius IX on December 8, 1854, holding that the Holy Virgin Mary, from the first instant of her conception, was preserved from all stain of original sin.

On November 26, 1895 Pope Leo XIII appointed Cyril Maqar as Coptic Catholic Patriarch of Alexandria with the name of Cyril II. This was seen by the orthodox Copts as an offence against their church, whose Pope Cyril II (1078–1092) was one of the great medieval theologians, famous for his thirty-four canons dealing with contemporary ethical issues and claiming to be the successor of Cyril I (412–444), the celebrated Coptic Orthodox Pope and saint prior to the Council of Chalcedon (451) in which the Western and Oriental churches parted.

The apostolic letter *Christi Domini* made the Coptic Catholic Church canonically legal in so far as it stated *Patriarcatum Alexanderinum restituimus et pro Coptis constituimus.*[73] The church was divided into three dioceses: the patriarchal diocese of Cairo and Lower Egypt; the diocese of Hermopolis Magna (Minya) and the diocese of Thebes (Luxor). In 1908 Cyril II was suspended which caused many Catholic Copts to return to their mother church. In 1922 Cyril II died in Beirut.

From 1908 to 1947 the Coptic Catholic Patriarchate was administered by two apostolic vicars, Maximus Sedfawi and later by Mark Khouzam. On August 9, 1947 Mark Khouzam was nominated patriarch. As Mark II he was enthroned on March 7, 1948, thus indicating that he was the successor of Mark the Apostle, seen by the Orthodox as the founder of their church and disregarding Popes Mark II (799–819), Mark III (1166–1189), Mark IV (1348–1363), Mark V (1610–1621), and Mark VI (1645–1660). Following his death on February 2, 1958, the synod of the Coptic Catholic bishops elected Stephanus I, whose nomination was approved by the See of Rome on June 17. He was enthroned on June 29, 1958. Stephanus I was the first Coptic Catholic patriarch of Alexandria elected to the Roman Catholic College of Cardinals on February 22, 1965. Due to ill-health and old age Stephanus I submitted his resignation. On June 9, 1986 the Holy Synod elected the former apostolic administrator (since February 24, 1984) and Bishop Andraos Ghattas of

Thebes (Luxor) as Stephanus II. He was enthroned on July 12, 1986 in the Church of the Lazarist Fathers in Alexandria.

The Coptic Catholic Patriarchate includes seven dioceses: the patriarchal diocese of Cairo and Lower Egypt; and the dioceses of Giza, Minya, Asyut, Sohag, Luxor, and Ismailiya.

The Coptic Catholic Eparchies

The Patriarchal Eparchy includes the region of Cairo with sixteen parishes; the region of the Delta with five parishes; and the region of Alexandria with twelve parishes. The parishes in Rome, Milan, Paris, New York (Brooklyn), Los Angeles, Montreal, Toronto, Sydney, and Melbourne also belong to the patriarchal eparchy.

The Eparchy of Giza was established on April 30, 2003 and includes Giza, the Fayyum, and Beni Suef with eleven parishes.

The Eparchy of Minya *(Hermopolis)* was established on November 26, 1895 by pontifical decree *Christi Domini*. It includes the region of Minya from Maghagha in the north to Dair Mawas. Dair Mawas and Mallawi were added on May 16, 1990. It includes twenty-seven parishes.

The Eparchy of Asyut *(Lycopolis)* was established on August 9, 1947. It extends from Dairut in the north to Sidfa in the south. The eparchy has thirty-nine parishes.

The Eparchy of Sohag was established on November 26, 1895 by pontifical decree *Christi Domini* of Leo XIII. The eparchy extends from Asyut to Luxor and includes twenty-one parishes.

The Eparchy of Thebes-Luxor was established on November 26, 1895 by pontifical decree *Christi Domini*. The episcopal see was once in Tahta, later in Sohag, finally in Luxor. It includes the regions of Qena, Aswan, the Red Sea, and Luxor and has twenty-one parishes.

The Eparchy of Ismailiya was established in January 1983 to include the Canal Zone, Sinai, and the eastern part of the Delta. It has twelve parishes.

The Rites of the Catholic Church in Egypt

The Catholic Church in Egypt reflects an unusual diversity and variety of Catholic communities which celebrate their religious rites according to their national and ethnic traditions. These are the Greek Melkites, the Maronites, the Syrian Catholics, the Chaldeans, the Armenian Catholics, the Latins, and as the largest group, the Coptic Catholics. All of these churches are an integral part of the Holy See of Rome.

The Greek-Melkite Catholic Patriarchate of Alexandria

Since the late eighteenth century, Catholic Melkites from Syria had settled in Egypt. In 1838 Pope Gregory XVI bestowed upon Maximus III Mazloum the title of Patriarch of Antioch, Alexandria, and Jerusalem. Today, Patriarch Gregory III Laham is Patriarch of Antioch, Alexandria, Jerusalem, and the whole Orient, and resides in Damascus. The General Patriarchal vicar for Egypt and the Sudan is Archbishop Joseph-Jules Zerey of Damietta. In Cairo, the patriarchate maintains the Cathedral of the Resurrection and six parishes, in Alexandria the Cathedral of the Dormition and three churches. Other churches are in Mansura and in Tanta.

The Maronite Diocese of Cairo

Ever since the seventeenth century, Maronite families are mentioned in Egypt. In the eighteenth century, Maronites had settled in Damietta, Zaqaziq, Old Cairo, Shubra, Heliopolis, Zeitun, and later in Mansura and the Canal Zone. In 1906 the Maronite Patriarch Hayek established a Patriarchal Vicariate in Egypt. In 1946, a Maronite diocese was established with the Cathedral of St. Joseph in Hamdi Street, Daher. In Shubra the Maronites have the Church of St. George, in Heliopolis the Church of St. Maron and the Chapel of St. Rita. The Maronite Church of St. Theresa is in Alexandria.

The Syrian Catholic Diocese of Cairo

Syrian Catholics have resided in Egypt since 1850. The Syrian Catholic Church of St. Elias dates from 1850. The Syrian Catholic Patriarch Ignace Pierre VIII Abdel Ahad resides in Beirut. The Syrian Catholic Bishop of Cairo is Mgr. Joseph Hannouche and resides at the Syrian Catholic Cathedral of the Rosary in 46 Daher Street. Other Syrian Catholic churches are in Heliopolis (St. Catherine) and in Alexandria (Sacred Heart).

The Chaldean Catholic Diocese of Cairo

The name 'Chaldean' was first applied by Pope Eugenius IV (fifteenth century) to those Assyrians (Eastern Syrians) who had accepted the teachings of the See of Rome. According to tradition, the Assyrian Church was founded by St. Thomas who had delegated his authority to Sts. Addai and

Mari. The first organizer of the Assyrian or Persian Church was Mar Aggain, Bishop of Seleucia-Ctesiphon in the third century. Toward the fifth century, the Assyrian Church adopted the teachings of Nestorius, Bishop of Constantinople. The Assyrian Church spread throughout the East as far as China, Mongolia, and Tibet.

In the eighth century, there was a sizable Assyrian (Nestorian) community in Egypt. Others resided in Cyprus and united with the See of Rome in 1445. In 1553, John Sulaka was invested as the first patriarch of the Chaldean Church by Pope Julius III.

The Chaldean Catholic community is Cairo was founded in 1891 by H.B. Patriarch Elias XIII Abu'l-Yunan who laid the foundation stone for the first Chaldean church which was later dedicated to St. Anthony. In 1950 Mgr. Emmanuel Rassam built a new church which the Chaldean Patriarch Joseph VII Ghanima dedicated to Our Lady of Fatima in 1953.

The Chaldean Patriarch resides in Baghdad. In addition to the Cathedral of Our Lady of Fatima in Heliopolis, the Chaldeans have the Church of St. Anthony the Great in Faggala and a parish in Alexandria.

The Armenian Catholic Patriarchate

The first attempts to unite the Armenian Orthodox Church with the Roman Catholic Church were begun in the twelfth century by Pope Eugenius III (1145–1153). It was not until the eighteenth century, through the work of the Capuchins, that a substantial part of the Armenian Church was united with Rome. In 1701 the first Armenian Catholic congregation was established in Constantinople. An unbroken line of Armenian Catholic Patriarchs dates from 1734. The Armenian Catholic Patriarch resides in Beirut. The patriarchate maintains the Church of St. Theresa in Heliopolis, the Cathedral of the Annunciation in Muhammad Sabri Abu 'Alam Street, and the Church of the Immaculate Conception in Alexandria.

The Armenian Catholics played an important role in the nineteenth century history of Egypt. During the reign of Muhammad 'Ali, Khosrov Cherakian (1808–1873) served as Muhammad 'Ali's secretary and interpreter Artin Bey Cherakian (1800–1859) was Minister of Foreign Affairs and Commerce.

The Apostolic Vicariate of Alexandria for the Latins in Egypt

The Apostolic Vicariate was established by Pope Gregory XVI in 1839 to serve the Latin (European) Catholics in Egypt and in the Arab World. The

Vicariate is headed by Bishop Bausordo who resides in Alexandria. For the African refugees there is an episcopal vicar in Cairo. The Cathedral of the Apostolic Vicariate is St. Catherine in Alexandria. In addition, there are twelve churches of the Latin rite in Alexandria, seventeen in Cairo, as well as churches in Damanhur, Port Said, Minya, Asyut, and Aswan. These churches are served by Franciscan, Salesian, Jesuit fathers and the Christian Brothers.

The Coptic Catholic Patriarchate of Alexandria (cf. p. 84)

The Assembly of Catholic Hierarchs in Egypt

This assembly was founded in 1992 to coordinate the work of the various Catholic rites in Egypt.

Catholic Congregations, Societies, and Orders of Monks Established in Egypt

There are 230 fathers of fourteen different orders:

The Franciscans of the Custody of the Holy Land, established in Jerusalem in the fourteenth century, have been represented in Alexandria and Cairo since 1682. Since the seventeenth century, the work of the Franciscans was divided into that of the Custody of the Holy Land with pastoral activities in Cairo and Lower Egypt, and the work of the Franciscans in Upper Egypt. This mission is known today as the Franciscan Vice-Province and became autonomous in 1992. The work of the Custody of the Holy Land includes the Center of Christian Oriental Studies, Muski, the Latin Cemetery in Old Cairo, and the parish of St. Joseph in Cairo. The Franciscan Vice-Province is the successor to the Egyptian Mission in Upper Egypt, established in 1697 by the *Propaganda fide*. The Franciscan Vice-Province maintains five churches in Cairo, nine in Alexandria, two in Buhaira, three in Gharbiya and the Canal Zone, and fourteen in Upper Egypt. The Franciscan Theological Seminary is in Giza. The seventy-four Franciscan fathers maintain thirty-six stations.

The Lazarists or the Congregation of Missions were established by St. Vincent de Paul in 1625. They arrived in Egypt in 1844. In Alexandria they have the church of the Miraculous Medal. Their monastery and School of St. Vincent is in Miami, Alexandria.

The Christian Brothers (Frères des Ecoles Chrétiennes), founded in 1684 by St. Jean de Baptiste de la Salle, arrived in Egypt in 1847. Together with the Lazarist fathers they opened their first school in Alexandria. Over the years they have established four colleges in Cairo, and two colleges in Alexandria. Their eleven fathers live in seven stations.

The Comboni Missionaries of the Sacred Heart of Jesus was founded by Father Daniel Comboni in 1867. In 1874 they transferred their work from Old Cairo to Cairo with the building of the Church of the Sacred Heart of Jesus. Additional centers were established in Zamalek, Helwan, and Aswan. In Sakakini they serve the Sudanese refugees. Their nineteen fathers maintain six stations.

The Society of African Missions was founded in Lyons in 1856 by Bishop Marion Brésillace. The first missionaries arrived in Egypt in 1877. In 1975 they turned over their missionary stations to the Apostolic Vicariate of the Delta. Today, their work is limited to the church of St. Mark in Shubra. Some of their fathers work with the Apostolic Vicariate. Sixteen fathers live in Shubra and Heliopolis.

The Society of Jesus, Jesuits was founded in 1538 by St. Ignatius of Loyola and approved in 1550. They arrived in Egypt between 1696 and 1744. In 1889 they established the College of the Holy Family in Faggala. Their College in Alexandria was established in 1882, and dedicated to St. Francis Xavier. Their house in Minya was opened in 1887, and the Church of the Holy Family in Matariya was dedicated in 1904. The mission in Garagos, north of Luxor, was opened in 1948. The twenty-five Jesuit Fathers maintain ten stations in Cairo, Alexandria, and Minya.

The Society of St. Francis of Sales, founded by St. John Bosco in 1841, established their work in Alexandria in 1896, Port Said in 1924, and Cairo in 1926 (the Salesian Institute in Rod al-Farag). In 1970, an agreement for technical and industrial cooperation between Italy and Egypt was signed, to be administered by the Salesian fathers. The twenty-nine Salesian fathers work in Rod al-Farag, Zeitun, and the Don Bosco Institute in Alexandria.

The Order of Mount Carmel or Carmelites were founded by St. Berthold in the twelfth century and reformed by St. John of the

Cross in the sixteenth century. They came to Egypt in 1926 where they maintain the church and the hospital of St. Theresa in Shubra and the Hospital of St. Theresa in Alexandria. Their seven fathers maintain three stations.

The Order of the Dominicans, founded by St. Dominic in 1215, established the Dominican Institute for Oriental Studies (IDEO) in 1928, at number 1 Masna' al-Tarabiche Street, Abbasiya. Father Anawati served as director of the institute from 1953 until his death in 1994. The ten fathers are attached to the institution.

The Fraternity of the Little Brothers of Jesus was established in 1933 by Father René Voillaume. In 1968, two brothers came to Cairo to work with the Institut Française d'Archéologie Orientale; others worked in Upper Egypt later. There are ten Little Brothers of Jesus working under the auspices of the Christian Association of Upper Egypt.

Prado is a society of diocesan priests and laymen, founded in 1860 by Father Antoine Chevrier of Lyons. Their purpose is to serve the poor in the spirit of Christ. They came to Egypt in 1974. Their fourteen fathers work in Asyut.

The Maryknoll Fathers were founded in 1911 in Hawthorne, USA. They arrived in Egypt in 1983 to work with young people in Maadi.

The Community of the Incarnate Word was founded in San Raffaele, Argentina, in 1984. Their purpose is the evangelization of their respective cultures. They came to Egypt in 1995 to work with the students of the Franciscan Theological Seminary in Giza. The five fathers live in Cairo, Alexandria, and Nassariya, Fayyum.

The Fathers of the Holy Trinity or Trinitarians were founded by St. John of Matha in Cerfroid, France in 1193 and approved in 1195 by Pope Innocent III. Their purpose was to liberate the Christian captives at the time of the Crusades. In 1599, they were reformed by St. Jean de Baptiste de Conception. In 1998 the Trinitarians established a mission to work with Sudanese refugees in Cairo. The four fathers live in Nasr City, Cairo.

The Assembly of the Superiors of the Major Institutions (ASMI) was founded in 1968 to coordinate the work of the various monastic orders and societies. They meet at the College of the Holy Family in Faggala.

Catholic Congregations, Societies, and Orders of Nuns Established in Egypt

There are forty different congregations with 1,103 sisters engaged in social, educational, and medical services throughout Egypt.

The Daughters of Charity of St. Vincent de Paul were founded in Paris on November 29, 1633. In 1844 seven sisters arrived in Alexandria to serve the poor by opening a dispensary and an orphanage. In 1901 they moved to Cairo, and in 1905 to the Canal Zone. In 1951, 1958, and 1996 they opened schools in Upper Egypt. An additional school was opened in Shibin al-Kom in 1997. Fifty-six sisters work at ten stations.

The Congregation of Our Lady of the Good Shepherd was founded by St. John Eudes in 1641. In 1845 Sister Marie Euphrasie and five sisters established themselves in the Muski with an orphanage and a school. At the request of Ferdinand de Lesseps, they established a hospital and a school in both Port Said and Suez, and additional institutions were founded in Minya, Fikreya, and Nag' al-Diq. Sixty-three sisters work at nine stations.

The Franciscan Missionary Sisters of the Immaculate Heart of Mary. On September 1859 six Italian Franciscan sisters arrived in Cairo to start a convent in Clot Bey. Over the years, additional stations were founded in Alexandria, the Delta, and Upper Egypt. They maintain fourteen schools and nine dispensaries. One hundred and five sisters work in fourteen houses.

The Missionary Sisters of the Nigrizia *(Pie Madri della Negrizia)* were founded by St. Daniel Comboni of Verona in 1872. They arrived in Egypt in 1887 to work in hospitals in Cairo, Alexandria, Edfu, and Aswan. They maintain fifteen stations with 136 sisters.

The Sisters of the Mother of God were founded in 1648 by Mgr. Oliver, the curate of Saint Sulpice. In 1880, upon request of the Khedive Tewfik, they engaged in educational work in Cairo and Alexandria. In their two stations they have seventeen sisters.

The Sisters of Our Lady of Sion were founded by Father Theodore Ratisbonne in 1843. They were called to Egypt where they opened schools for girls in Cairo and Alexandria in 1880, and later in Minya. They have three houses with seven sisters.

The Congregation of the Sisters of Our Lady of the Apostles was founded by Father Augustin Planque in 1876 to work in social, educational, and medical fields. They maintain stations in Cairo, Alexandria, Girga, Mallawi, Mahalla al-Kubra, and Tanta. Forty-six sisters serve in their eleven stations.

The Sisters of Mercy of St. Charles Borromaeus were founded in 1659. Father Ladislaus Schneider, established this congregation's work in Egypt in 1884, where the sisters were engaged in educational and nursing activities. They maintain a convent with kindergarten in Maadi and schools in Cairo (Bab al-Luq) and Alexandria, as well as a home for the aged. Their thirty sisters live in four stations.

The Dominican Missionary Sisters of Our Lady of Help were founded in Martinique in 1868 by the Sisters Laure and Hermance Sabès. In 1891 they started a school in Faggala, in 1912 a hospital in Port Said, and in 1921 a school and a dispensary in Heliopolis. The twenty sisters live in three stations.

The Missionary Daughters of Our Lady of Sorrows of Tarbes (France) were founded by Mother St. Jean-Baptiste and Canon Dominique Ribes in March 1866. They arrived in Egypt in 1891 and established a home for the aged in Shubra and other centers in Alexandria and Heliopolis. Their thirteen sisters live in two stations.

The Congregation of the Franciscan Sisters of the Immaculate Conception was founded by Sister Marie Ignace of Jesus of Belle Prairie in the United States in 1873. Their first mission in Egypt was established in 1898 in Fayyum, 1899 in Damanhur, 1922 in Cairo, and later in Alexandria, Abu Kir, Shibin al-Kom, and Qesna. Their College of St. Claire is directed by the Sisters of the Rosary of Jerusalem. Their mission in Fayyum is under the supervision of the Coptic Sisters of Jesus and Mary. There are two sisters living in the secondary school of the Sacred Heart in Roushdy, Alexandria.

The Society of the Sacred Heart was founded in Paris by St. Marie Madelaine S. Barat for the glorification of the Sacred Heart of Christ. In 1908 the sisters opened their first school in Ghamra, and in 1911 another in Heliopolis. Following the Vatican Council II they collaborated with Association of Upper Egypt Educational Development (AUEED) for the education of women in Upper Egypt, in Abu Qurqas, Bayadeya, Beni Ebeid, Samalut, and Dairut. Their forty-seven sisters live in ten stations.

The Sisters of the Holy Family was founded in 1922 by St. Emile de Rodat of Villefranche-de-Rouergue in France. Since 1894 the sisters work in the Middle East. In Mansura they direct a College of the Holy Family, where five sisters live.

The Congregation of the Franciscan Sisters of Christ the King was founded in Maribor, Yugoslavia, in 1869. In 1912 they began their work with young women in Cairo, and later in Alexandria. Their ten sisters live in Cairo and Alexandria.

The Congregation of the Sisters of Charity of Besançon was founded in 1799 by St. Jeanne Antide Thouret. They arrived in Egypt in 1909 to work among young impoverished girls and women. They maintain schools and dispensaries. A center for the handicapped was opened in 1992. They have work in Alexandria, Cairo, Tenth of Ramadan, Dair al-Ganadla, Shaikh Zein al-Din, Asyut, Tahta, and Nag' Hammadi. Their twenty-three sisters live in seven stations.

The Sisters of St. Joseph of Lyons, founded by Father Medaille. in 1650, arrived in Egypt in 1907 to work in educational and medical projects, also cooperating with Caritas-Egypt. Their twelve sisters have stations in Cairo, Minya, and Asyut.

The Congregation of the Egyptian Sisters of the Sacred Heart is the first Coptic Catholic congregation of sisters, founded in 1913 in Tahta by Mother Marie Margurite Sebeillet. Between 1913 and 2004, they have established nine schools and seven social centers. They have twenty-two houses with 160 sisters.

The Armenian Sisters of the Immaculate Conception was founded by Cardinal Anton-Pierre IX Hassoun in Constantinople in 1847. In 1913 they came to Alexandria, in 1937 to Cairo, and in 1953 they established a school in Heliopolis. Their five sisters live in Heliopolis.

The Congregation of the Sisters of Mt. Carmel, the Holy Family in Exile and St. Theresa of Avila was established in 1247, and reformed in the sixteenth century. The Carmelite sisters arrived in Egypt in November 1927 and established themselves in Matariyah. They are a contemplative community. They have had a convent in the Fayyum since 1996. Their ten sisters live in the Fayyum.

The Congregation of the Daughters of Marie Auxiliatrice, also known as the Salesian Sisters of St. John Bosco was founded in Piémont, Italy in 1872. In 1916 they began their work in

Alexandria, and in 1927 in Heliopolis. The Salesian Institute in Rod al-Farag was inaugurated in 1929. The twenty-one sisters live in three houses.

The Order of the Poor Claires was founded in 1212 by St. Clara under the direction of St. Francis of Assisi. They arrived in Egypt in 1919 and they work in Alexandria with nine sisters.

The Franciscan Missionary Sisters of Mary, founded in 1877 by Hélène de Chappotin de Neuville, came to Egypt in 1924 for educational work. They established schools in Cairo (Zamalek), Alexandria (Bulkley and Cleopatra), Luxor, and Kom Ombo. Their twenty-seven sisters live in five stations.

The Carmelite Sisters of St. Joseph, founded in 1872 by Mother Marguerite Marie du Sacré Coeur, came to Egypt in 1931 where they maintained elementary schools in Cairo and in Nekhela. They also have work in Abu Tig and Asyut. Their seventeen sisters live in three stations.

The Congregation of the Franciscan Sisters of Elisabeth, founded in 1828 by Mother Elisabeth Vendramini and Father Luigi Moran, came to Egypt in 1935 to work mainly in Upper Egypt, in Tawirat, Qena, Naqada, and Maghagha. They opened social centers and dispensaries. In Cairo they work with Caritas-Egypt in Kafr al-Sisi (Pyramids). Their regional convent is in Giza. They have sixty-two sisters in twelve stations.

The Society of Our Lady Marie was founded in Bordeaux in 1667. They follow the spirituality of St. Ignatius of Loyola through contemplation and religious studies. They offer their services to the church in Egypt in their respective vocations. The six sisters live in Daher, Cairo.

The Sisters of Our Lady of Perpetual Help were founded in Harissa, Lebanon by H.B. Maximos Seyegh. They came to Egypt in 1945 to help the Melkite community in Heliopolis where they operate a school. The seven sisters live in Heliopolis.

The Fraternity of the Little Sisters of Jesus of Charles de Foucauld began in 1939. They are "contemplative sisters in the world" and work in Daher, Cairo, Ezbet al-Qusayarin, Muqattam, and the Fayyum. Their fifteen sisters live in four stations.

The Little Sisters of the Sacred Heart, founded in 1902 in Poggio a Caiano, Florence, came to Egypt in 1953 to assist the Franciscan Mission in Kafr al-Dawar (1978), Abu Tig (1996), and Luxor (1997). In Esna they maintain a school. Their seventeen sisters live in Cairo, Kafr al-Dawar, Abu Tig, and Esna.

The Coptic Sisters of Jesus and Mary, established by the Coptic Sisters of the Sacred Heart in 1969 were recognized in April 1975. They operate kindergartens and primary schools in Sakakini, Heliopolis Damietta, Medinet Nasr, Zaqaziq, Medinet al-Salam, and Hurghada. The fifty-six sisters live in nine stations.

The Sisters of Providence, were founded in Montreal, Canada, under the direction of Bishop Ignatius Bourget of Montreal. Bishop Isaac Ghattas requested them to work in the hospital in Minya. The sisters operate a dispensary and assist poor girls and women. The three sisters live in one house.

The Missionary Sisters of Charity of Mother Theresa of Calcutta arrived in Egypt 1988 to work among the poor, regardless of religion, in Faggala, Muqattam, Alexandria, and Asyut. The twenty-eight sisters live in four houses.

The Apostolic Indian Congregation of the Daughters of Mary, founded in 1938 by Bishop Joseph Kuzhinjalil, came to Cairo upon request of the Melkite Patriarch Maximus V Hakim. They work in the Greek-Catholic school in Heliopolis. The three sisters live in Heliopolis.

The Franciscan Sisters of the Cross of Lebanon, founded by a Lebanese Capuchin in 1930, were called by Patriarch Stephanus II Ghattas to administer the homes for retired clergy in Maadi (1988), and in Abu Kir (1996), Alexandria. The seven sisters live in Cairo and in Alexandria.

The Lebanese Basilian Sisters, founded in 1834, came to Egypt in 1988 to work in the Old Peoples' Home in Helwan where the four sisters also live.

The Columbian Missionary Sisters of St. Theresa, founded in 1929 in Santa Rosa di Osus, Columbia, came to Egypt in 1991 to work in Shubra, Alexandria, and Kom Buha (Dairut). The nine sisters maintain three stations.

The Sisters of the Rosary of Jerusalem, founded in 1855 in Jerusalem, came to Cairo in 1991 to work with the Apostolic Nuntius and in the College of St. Claire in Heliopolis. The six sisters live in Zamalek and Heliopolis.

The Daughters of St. Anne, founded in Piacenza in 1866, have worked in the Franciscan Theological Seminary in Giza since 1999. Some of the sisters are attached to the Catholic bishop of Minya. The nine sisters live in Zeitun and Minya.

The Sisters of the Incarnate Word are the feminine branch of the Congregation of the Incarnate Word, founded in Argentina in 1988. The sisters came to Egypt upon the request of the Apostolic Vicar to work in the Old Peoples' Home in Chatby, Alexandria. The fifteen sisters live in Cairo and Alexandria.

The Canossa Sisters, founded in Verona by Sister Magdalene Canossa in 1808, came to Egypt in 2001. They work with the Sudanese refugees in Sakakini, Maadi, and with the Philippine emigrants in Cairo. The eight sisters live in Daher and Helmiet al-Zeitun.

The Sisters of Maria Bambina were founded in 1832 to serve the poor, especially children. The seven sisters live in Port Said and in al-Qantara-West.

The Union of the Mothers Superior of the Religious Orders is situated at the College of the Sacred Heart, Ghamra, and coordinates the work or the various religious congregations in Egypt.

Theological Differences between the Coptic Orthodox Church and the Roman Catholic Church

Ever since the fifteenth century, Roman Catholic popes have tried to persuade the Oriental Orthodox Churches (the Copts, Syrians, and Armenians) to accept the teachings of the See of Rome. The attempts of the Council of Ferrara and Florence (1438–1445) had produced important papal documents,[74] and the theological expectations toward a more positive understanding. But an organic union with the Roman Catholic Church remained unfulfilled. True, through the Council of Ferrara in 1438, the Catholic church had won back some of the prestige which the papacy had lost, and the pope of Rome had appeared as the leader of Christendom again.

The real theological problems remained unsolved. These included the Roman Catholic belief in purgatory; the employment of unleavened bread in the eucharist; the liturgical issue of the use of the epiclesis in the eucharist; the inclusion of the *filioque* in the Nicene-Constantinopolitan

Creed; and above all, of course, the papal claims to absolute supremacy. Long disputes ensued about some of the issues, and here and there a temporary compromise was reached as in the case of the *filioque*, but with the doctrine of the double procession of the Holy Spirit from the Father *through* the Son, no concrete results were reached.

Theological discussions for a better ecumenical understanding between Christians of the various churches actually began in 1948 when the Coptic Orthodox Church joined the World Council of Churches in Amsterdam as one of its founding members. The official dialogues with the other orthodox took place in 1964 (Aarhus), 1967 (Bristol), 1970 (Geneva), and 1971 (Addis Ababa), while the discussions with the Roman Catholic Church commenced in 1971 in Vienna. In May 1973 Pope Shenuda III and Pope Paul VI signed the most significant Christological agreement in the Vatican, an issue that had separated the Coptic Orthodox Church from the Roman Catholic and the Byzantine orthodox churches since the Council of Chalcedon in 451. In citing the Vienna agreement, the two popes followed the Christology of the Alexandrian pope and theologian Cyril I: "We believe that our Lord, God and Savior Jesus Christ is the Incarnate Word of God. We believe that He was perfect in His Divinity and perfect in His Humanity, and that His Divinity never departed from His Humanity not even a single instant nor a twinkle of an eye."[75]

Six Pro-Oriente consultations between the Coptic Orthodox Church and the Roman Catholic Church were held in Europe and in Egypt between 1971 and 1991. However, the following issues still separate the two apostolic churches:

The *filioque*, the procession of the Holy Spirit from the Father and the Son, arises as a liturgical problem in the text of the Nicene-Constantinopolitan creed. As such it has remained a matter of dispute. The principal objection of the Copts to the filioque had been based on its implication of two 'sources' and thus of two 'principles of origin' in the Godhead. To the Orthodox, the *filioque* is a fundamental violation of the Trinitarian theology. Moreover, the biblical texts denouncing the *filioque* are abundantly clear (John 14:16; 15:36).

The issue of purgatory, the state of suffering after death in which the souls of those who die in venial sin and of those who still owe some debt of temporal punishment for mortal sin, are rendered fit to enter heaven. Such souls are helped by prayers and alms, and other good works of the living.

At the Council of Florence (1439), the Roman Catholics demanded that the Orthodox accept the doctrine of purgatory as apostolic teaching, binding on all Christians. Clement of Alexandria (second century) had asserted that those who have repented on their deathbed and had no time to perform works of penance in this life would be sanctified in the next by a purifying fire (Stromateis 7.6). For the Copts, prayers on behalf of the dead are an apostolic tradition, but this did not imply a doctrine of purgatory. The liturgy always included prayers for those who had fallen asleep in faith, though this said nothing about them in an intermediate state from which they would eventually, through cleansing, be translated to heaven. Even the biblical reference does not prove purgatory.[76]

The orthodox critics, ever since the eleventh century, have fastened upon the issue of azymes as proof that the Roman Catholics actually followed Mosaic laws in their Eucharistic liturgy. Those who use unleavened bread, so it was said, were still under the shadow of the law. Paraphrasing Galatians 5:23, it was argued that anyone who kept azymes was bound to keep the whole law, so that "if you eat unleavened bread, Christ will be of no advantage to you." The anathema of the apostle upon circumcision and Sabbath observance also applied to the *azymites* (those who administer the eucharist with unleavened bread). Orthodox theologians have sought to prove that Christ had instituted the Lord's Supper with leavened bread. After all, the leaven constituted a symbol of the Kingdom of God (Matthew 13:33; Luke 13:21).

The use of the *epiclesis*, the prayer that God may send His Holy Spirit upon the sacrifice (the eucharist) so as to make the bread to be the body of Christ and the cup to be the blood of Christ was under dispute. Partly as a result of Eucharistic controversies during the ninth and eleventh centuries, the Roman Catholics maintain that it was the repetition of the words of institution: "This is my Body" and "This is my Blood" that effected the sacramental miracle of changing bread and wine into the body and blood of Christ. Although it was decreed at the Council of Florence (1439) that by the power of the words of Christ, the substance of the bread and the wine is converted into the body and blood of Christ, orthodox theologians continued the liturgical practice of the *epiclesis* and the doctrinal stand derived from this prayer.

Repeatedly, Roman Catholics have criticized the orthodox for failing to mix water with the wine in the celebration of the Eucharist. The use of water with the wine was to remind the believer that at the crucifixion of Christ "the soldier pierced his side with a spear, and at once their came out blood and water" (John 19:34).

The Orthodox Copts practice a devout piety and an elaborate cult honoring the Mother of God with eight major feasts.[78] In addition, every twenty-first day of each month is dedicated to the Holy Virgin. The Assumption of the Holy Virgin is the major Coptic Marian feast, which falls on Misra 16 (August 22). Pope Peter I of Alexandria declared in 311 that she is the *Aeiparthenos*, the simpler *virgin*, who retained her virginity prior, during, and after the birth of the Savior, according to the teaching of Pope Peter I of Alexandria, 311.

Contemporary Roman Catholic Mariology, which reflects late medieval, nineteenth, and twentieth century mariological developments, appear strange in the light of the Coptic veneration of the Mother of God. This pertains to the dogma of the Immaculate Conception, defined by Pope Pius IX on December 8, 1845. This holds that the Holy Virgin, from the instant of her conception, was, by a most singular grace of God, in view of the merits of Jesus Christ, preserved from all stain of Original Sin. This doctrine is revealed by God, and therefore to be firmly and steadfastly believed by all the faithful.[79] It is one of those ambivalent incidents in the history of religion that the image of the Immaculata, as she had appeared to Cathérine Labouré of the Filles de la Charité in Paris in 1830, became the most popular devotional icon of the Holy Virgin among the orthodox Copts, following her apparition at the dome of the Church of the Holy Virgin in Zeitun on April 2, 1968.

While the Copts commemorate the Dormition on Tuba 21, or January 29, and the Assumption of the Holy Virgin on Misra 16, or August 22, they have no explicit dogma stating the miraculous reunion of her soul with her body in heaven as proclaimed by Pope Pius XII on November 1, 1950. Two Catholic nineteenth-century devotionals have impressed themselves upon the piety of some Upper-Egyptian Copts. These are the images of the Sacred Heart of Jesus and those of the Sacred and Immaculate Heart of Mary. In 1898, the Coptic Catholic Church was dedicated to the Sacred Heart of Jesus, the feast being on the Friday after the Octave of Corpus Christi.[80]

Undoubtedly the main obstacle for a mutual understanding between the Pope of Alexandria and the Pope of Rome is the result of the First

Vaticanum in July 1870 that affirmed as "divinely revealed dogma" not only the papal primacy established by Christ in the person of St. Peter (Matthew 16:18, 19), but also his infallibility when he speaks *ex cathedra* in matters of faith and morals. Thus infallibility is the guaranty against error in the matter of dogma and morality.[81] On the day of voting, 601 members were present, 451 voted *placet*; 150 rejected the *placet*.

The Episcopal Church in Egypt

Historical Note

The Episcopal Church in Egypt, an integral part of the Anglican Communion, is an outgrowth of the work of the Church Missionary Society (CMS). The evangelical movement in the Church of England took missionaries from the Church Missionary Society in 1799, under the guidance of John and Thomas Scott, and formed the Society for Missions to Africa and the East. From its inception, this society maintained cordial relations with the missionary societies of the nonconformist churches. In continental Europe, for example, there was the Basel Mission, which was founded in 1815, and drew support from Germany and Switzerland.

The CMS sent the Revered William Jowett to Egypt in 1818, where he was welcomed by Coptic priests and monks. Toward the end of 1825 the Basel Mission, also working in Africa, commissioned five men to work in Egypt. These were the pastors Mueller, Kruse, Kugler, Lieder, and Samuel Gobat, who later became the second Evangelical Lutheran Bishop of Jerusalem from 1846–1879. Pastor J.R.T. Lieder of the Basel Mission remained in Egypt until 1865 as German consular chaplain, though the work of the mission was practically closed in 1862.

Prior to his consecration as Pope Cyril IV in 1854, Father Daoud al-Antoni, while residing in Bush, was a regular visitor to the Bible classes of the Reverend Lieder. Several of the orthodox co-workers were trained by CMS missionaries. The first CMS mission started small schools for boys in six towns where evangelical services were held with orthodox Copts in attendance.

The Church Missionary Society from 1882–1952

Following the occupation of Egypt by the British forces under Sir Garnet Wolseley in the summer and fall of 1882 a new situation emerged for foreign missions. From 1882 to 1914 the khedive remained the legal authority within the Ottoman Empire, though in reality from 1882–1907 Lord Evelyn B. Cromer was the ruler of the country. Following several appeals by Miss Whately, the CMS determined to resume their missionary work in Egypt, though this time with a special mandate to bring the Gospel to the Muslims.

The medical work was begun by Dr. Harpur who founded in 1889 the CMS hospital in Old Cairo that was named after him. A little later, a branch of this hospital was opened in Menuf in the province of Minufiya. The educational work centered around five schools, two of which were in Old Cairo, two in Menuf, and one school in Bulaq. Thirteen village schools were handed over to the Coptic Orthodox Church.

In July 1952, the time was ripe for a transfer of the CMS's missionary institutions to the indigenous Episcopal Church of Egypt.

The Churches and Centers of the Episcopal Church

The Episcopal churches in Egypt are: All Saints' Cathedral at 5 Michel Lutfalla, Zamalek, which offers services in English, Amharic, Dinka, and Nuer for Sudanese and other refugees. The new Episcopal Cathedral of All Saints' in Zamalek was consecrated in 1988, after the former cathedral situated on Corniche al-Nil was demolished to construct the Sixth of October Bridge across the Nile. Their other churches are: in Alexandria the churches of St. Mark and All Saints'; in Port Said the Church of the Epiphany; in Giza the Church of the Good Shepherd; in Old Cairo the Church of Jesus the Light of the World; in Maadi the Church of St. John the Baptist; in Menuf the Church of St. Mark; in Heliopolis the Church of St. Michael and All Archangels; and in Suez the Church of the Savior Christ.

The Episcopal Church maintains social and development centers in Heliopolis, Bulaq, Medinet al-Salam; al-Nahda; Menuf; Ras al-Suda; and Alexandria. For example: the School for the Deaf is in Old Cairo; the Harpur Memorial Hospital (founded in 1910) in Menuf; and the polyclinic and a Community Health Center in Sadat City, which is a developing industrial area between Cairo and Alexandria.

The Episcopal diocese of Egypt includes churches serving Anglican and international congregations in Tunis, Tunisia (St. George); Tripoli, Libya (Christ the King); Asmara, Eritrea (St. George); Addis Ababa, Ethiopia (St.

Matthew's). The Right Reverend Dr. Munir Hanna Anis is the Episcopal Bishop of Egypt with North Africa and the Horn of Africa. The diocese is part of the Archdiocese of Jerusalem.

The Theological Differences between the Coptic Orthodox Church and the Episcopal Church in Egypt

From October 7–11, 1985 the Anglican churches had invited representatives of the Oriental orthodox churches to convene at St. Albans to discuss matters of theological agreement. The issue of the Anglican ordination of women to the priesthood was already the chief topic of discussion. On October 1, 1987 the Most Reverend Robert Runcie, Archbishop of Canterbury, met with Pope Shenuda III at the Monastery of St. Bishoi. Theological agreement was reached on the creed of Nicea-Constantinople without the *filioque*, which was the first time a Western church accepted the omission of the *filioque* clause in the creed. Other agreements included the Christological formula of St. Cyril on the "one nature of the Word of God Incarnate."

At the 1988 Lambeth Conference, the bishops' gathering of the twenty-seven provinces of the Anglican Communion every ten years, the ordination of women even to the episcopate was recognized. Pope Shenuda III had sent Metropolitan Bishoi to attend the conference to present the Coptic position on the issues condemning homosexuality, polygamy, and the ordination of women. The same issues were discussed at an Anglican-Oriental Orthodox forum at the Monastery of St. Bishoi from March 12–16, 1990. In spite of the doctrinal agreements as to the Trinity and the Christology, the issues of women's ordination, homosexuality (especially among the clergy), and the use of the historical-critical approach to the Holy Scriptures constitute real problems for mutual understanding and cooperation.

The Episcopal Church in Egypt adheres to a conservative biblical position, has not ordained women to the priesthood, and rejects any form of homosexuality.

The Evangelical Churches in Egypt

The Beginnings of the Evangelical Mission in Egypt

The Mission of Peter Heyling of Lübeck (1633–1634)

Little is known of the life and work of Peter Heyling, the first evangelical missionary to Egypt, and later to Ethiopia.

Peter Heyling, the son of a goldsmith from the Hanseatic City of Lübeck, was born in either 1607 or 1608, at a time which marked the prelude to the contest of arms between Protestants and Catholics. The rival parties had begun to muster their strength, and in 1608, a Protestant League of German princes was founded, to be followed by the formation of a Catholic League in 1609. Heyling attended the gymnasium in Lübeck, where he was educated in the doctrines of the Evangelical Lutheran Church, which he wholeheartedly accepted. Already early in his life, the young student felt the call to share his religious convictions and to propagate the truth as he saw it.[82] He studied the writing of Martin Luther (1483–1546), Johann Arndt (1555–1621), Johann Tauler (1300–1361), and Thomas à Kempis (1380–1471), which unquestionably left a profound impression upon the young Heyling. By this time, the Thirty Years' War was in full swing, and in 1627 and 1628, Germany, and especially Northern Germany and the Hanseatic cities, became increasingly involved in the violence of the contending forces. The famous siege of Stralsund occurred from February to August 1628, in which the citizens compelled the hitherto unconquered Wallenstein Army to retire. In 1628, at the age of twenty, Heyling left Lübeck in order to study law in Paris.

While in Paris, Heyling joined a small circle of seven friends, all of whom aimed at the fulfillment of the evangelical injunction to go out into the world and to preach the Gospel of Jesus Christ. Their goal was the rejuvenation of the ancient Eastern Orthodox Churches, which according to their judgment, had departed from the evangelical truth. Also in Paris he met with Hieronymus von Dorne, who like Heyling ventured toward the Orient, traveling to Jerusalem by way of Malta, Constantinople, and Syria. In 1634, Heyling met von Dorne in the Holy City.

He sailed from Malta, and reached Alexandria three weeks later, in the spring of 1633. During the seventeenth century, the Coptic Orthodox Church was to a great extent inert, whereas the Latin Church concentrated its efforts to unite the Copts with the See of Rome. Politically, Murad IV (1623–1640) ruled Egypt through eight pashas, and for the Christians it was a time of exactions and afflictions. Arriving from Europe, it was only natural, then, that Heyling would be met by members of the Latin Church, probably by the Capuchin fathers, to whom Egypt had been entrusted by the newly founded (1622) *Congregatio de Propaganda Fides*. Owing to his pronounced evangelical tenets, Heyling was received with a certain amount of distrust, though his biographer does not fail to impress upon the reader that in theological disputes Heyling was considerate and moderate with regard to his opponents, without, however, abandoning his evangelical position.

While in Alexandria, Heyling was offered hospitality by the French consul, until he was invited by a French merchant to sail with him to Cairo on his boat. On arriving in Cairo, he stayed with this merchant, who also supplied him with Turkish dress. For the execution of his missionary plans, Heyling realized that he had to study Arabic. Having consulted the merchant, he was advised, especially since he had no money, to enter one of the four Coptic Orthodox monasteries in the Wadi al-Natrun. Here, he was informed that he would be able to learn the language.

In April 1633, "guided by the Lord," Heyling set out for the the Monastery of St. Macarius (Dair Abu Maqar), in order to study Arabic and in exchange to acquaint the Coptic Desert Fathers with the doctrines of the Lutheran Reformation. In those days, the only way to get to the monasteries was by sailing on the Rosetta Branch of the Nile from Bulaq to al-Terrana, and from there either by donkey or camel across the desert.

In the meantime, however, the Capuchin fathers had approached a certain Barsum, who was second to the Coptic Patriarch, and also in the service of the Turkish Pasha, and had accused Heyling of heresy. The priests suggested to Barsum, that the heretic should be taken to Alexandria, in order to be expelled from Egypt.

During his stay in the Monastery of Abu Maqar, which at that time was occupied by by between ten and fourteen monks, three Arab mercenaries came to the monastery to arrest Heyling. After reading the warrant, Heyling hurried into the monastery chapel in order to evade the Arabs. Thy followed him, and demanded that he leave the monastery and return to Alexandria. Heyling, however, sent the mercenaries back and remained in the desert.

In answer to a letter from the anonymous French merchant, after three months' stay in the monastery, Heyling returned to Cairo, where he engaged again in a theological disputation in defence of his evangelical belief. Later, he was introduced to an old and pious Syrian archbishop, who promised him that within twenty days he could join the monks of the Monastery of the Syrians, who were coming to Cairo to fetch the monastic supplies. During this time, Heyling visited the Syrian archbishop daily, so as to learn the Syriac language. His Latin opponents, however, went to the Syrian archbishop, warned him of Heyling's heresies, and requested that he prevent Heyling from returning to the desert. The archbishop replied that he had seen neither evil nor anything un-Christian in Heyling, and since the desert was the *locus Christi*, he could not hinder any Christian who wanted to go there. Thus, in the Name of God, Heyling went for the second time to the Wadi al-Natrun, but this time to the two monasteries which are situated close to each other. These, of course, could only have been the Monasteries of St. Bishoi and that of the Syrians, also known as the Monastery of the Holy Virgin and St. John Kame. Altogether, Heyling remained in the desert for five months, staying in one monastery three months, and in the other for two. In the Monastery of the Syrians, Heyling met both Syrian monks and other nationalities, and saw a very ancient Syriac library.

By Easter 1634, Heyling had returned to Cairo to join a group of Syrian and Coptic pilgrims to Jerusalem. In the fall of the same year he accompanied an ecclesiastical delegation from Cairo to Ethiopia, where he stayed at the royal court in Gondar where the kings Susenius and Fasilides resided. Heyling worked as theologian and educator in Ethiopia until 1652. He was permitted to return to Cairo, but en route at the Sudanese Red Sea port of Suakin, the local pasha believed him to be a spy and beheaded him.

The Moravian Evangelical Mission in Egypt (1750–1785)

The Moravian Brethren or Moravian Church was founded in the east of Bohemia, soon after the death of John Huss in 1415. As pre-Reformation Protestants they taught the Apostles Creed, rejected purgatory, the worship of saints, and the primacy of the Pope of Rome. They practiced infant baptism, confirmation, and the Lord's Supper. Under the leadership of Count Zinzendorf, a fervent Lutheran and follower of the pietist Spener, many eighteenth century Moravian Brethren had accepted the Lutheran teachings.

In the middle of the eighteenth century the Brethren of Herrenhut commissioned the medical doctor Johannes Rüfer to serve in Egypt. However, on account of extreme travel difficulties, exertions, and hardship, he died in Egypt. In 1750, Friedrich Wilhelm Hocker, a young medical student, was sent to Cairo. For several years he resided in Cairo where he ministered as a physician and studied Arabic. In the course of his stay he presented his credentials, written by Count Zinzendorf, to the Coptic Orthodox Pope Mark VII (1745–1769). Some time later, in December 1753 the Coptic pope replied to the German count's letter. While in Cairo, Hocker translated several sermons and speeches, as well as some of the hymns by Zinzendorf, into Arabic.

The watchmaker John Antes, originally from the U.S.A, had joined the Moravian Brethren in Egypt. As a violinist and composer of chamber music, his services enriched Moravian worship. In 1779 he was attacked by some Arab notables who wanted to blackmail him. He finally returned to Europe in 1781 where he died in 1811.

The carpenter Johann Heinrich Danke proceeded to Upper Egypt where he worked in the village of al-Bahnasa, south of Beni Suef. Every year he used to spend several months in the village. In 1772 he died in Cairo and was buried in the vault of the Greek Orthodox Church of St. George in Old Cairo. Some other brethren continued the work of Danke for eight more years. In 1780 three additional missionaries from Germany arrived in Cairo to work in "the field of the Lord." Hocker died in 1782 and in the following year the Moravian mission in Egypt was discontinued.[83]

The Coptic Evangelical Synod of the Nile

Historical Note

In May 1853, the General Synod of the United Presbyterian Church of North America decided in its meeting in Allegheny to send some of the missionaries operating in Syria to serve in Egypt. The first missionary and his wife arrived in Cairo on November 15, 1854. By 1861, a total of seven missionaries had established themselves, with their wives.

The first American missionaries to Egypt were Dr. and Mrs. Thomas McCague and Dr. James Barnett. They were soon joined by Dr. John Hogg, Dr. Julian Lansing, Dr. Andrew Watson (father of Dr. Charles Watson, founder of the American University in Cairo), and others. Great emphasis was laid on the establishment and operation of good schools, Bible teaching and distribution, and a preaching ministry based in several major cities, but also carried on in many villages largely by means of house-boat travel up and down the Nile. Medical work and an expanded Christian literature program were subsequently added. Scores of schools were eventually opened throughout the Delta and the Nile Valley. In 1860, the missionaries organized themselves into a presbytery under the authority of the General Assembly in America. In 1863, the first congregation was organized and the following year a School of

Religion was opened. In 1871, again on authority of the General Assembly, the missionaries organized themselves into a Mission Association, concerned strictly with the program and problems of the mission, thus opening the way for the infant national church to grow with a large measure of independence. By the turn of the century there were four presbyteries. Today there are eight. Over these was the authority of the Synod of the Nile, an integral part of the United Presbyterian Church of North America until it was granted permission to withdraw in 1957. Financially independent for many years, except for several cooperative projects, the Coptic Evangelical Church, in 1926, assumed full responsibility for the Theological Seminary.

The Coptic Evangelical Synod of the Nile belongs to the Evangelical Reform churches and accepted in 1932 the "Confessional Statement" of 1929, which is a revision of the Westminster Confession of 1646. The church accepts the canonical books of the Holy Scriptures without the Old Testament Apocrypha. For matters of faith and order the church relies upon the "Confessional Statement." The church does accept the *filioque*.

The Structures of the Synod of the Nile

The Coptic Evangelical Synod of the Nile has 312 congregations in Lower and Upper Egypt which are served by 261 pastors. The Synod of the Nile is divided into eight presbyteries.

The **Delta Presbytery** has conference centers in Port Said, Ismailiya, and Qanater; and schools in Autrin, Port Said, Qanater, Mansura, Tanta, and Benha.

The **Cairo Presbytery** with the Synod offices in Ezbekiya, and the offices of the Coptic Evangelical Organization for Social Services (CEOSS) in Nuzha Gedida, also has the Evangelical Theological Seminary in Abbasiya, the Fowler Orphanage and conference center, and centers in Helwan and Shubra Sharqiya. Other schools are Ramses College and the New Ramses College (formerly the American College for Girls), the Nile Synod School, and the Salam School. Their medical services include the Ezbekiya Hospital, and clinics in Helwan and Giza.

The **Wasta Presbytery** has conference centers in the Fayyum and Maghagha, and schools in Beni Suef, Maghagha, and Fayyum.

The **Minya Presbytery** has its center in the important Second Evangelical church in Minya with three schools and a conference center in Etsa.

The **Mallawi Presbytery** maintains schools in al-Qusiya, Mallawi, Dairut, Hawatka, and Bayadiya.

The **Asyut Presbytery**, heir of a distinguished Presbyterian missionary heritage has Asyut College, founded in 1865 by Dr. John Hogg, the Pressly Memorial Institute (PMI) also of 1865, and the Asyut Hospital, opened in 1868. Today, the Asyut Presbytery maintains four schools.

The **Sohag Presbytery** operates two schools in Sohag.

The **al-'Aliya Presbytery** has four conference centers in Luxor, Besna, Bendara, and Beqna. The Presbytery operates three schools in Luxor and one in Beqna. The Hospital of the German Evangelical Mission of Upper Egypt in Aswan is administered by the Coptic Evangelical Synod of the Nile. This hospital is situated on the east bank of the Nile next to the Grand Hotel, Aswan.

The beginnings of the German Evangelical Mission in Upper Egypt, formerly the German Sudan Pioneer Mission, go back to 1900. The work commenced with the opening of a school in Aswan, and in 1901, a clinic was opened. The hospital was dedicated in 1911. In 1960, a new hospital wing, as well as a nurses' home, were added to the existing buildings.

In addition to their work in Aswan, the German Evangelical Mission has maintained a station at Daraw, nine kilometers south of Kom Ombo, since 1907.

The Other Evangelical Churches

The Holiness Churches are divided into numerous groups. Many of them arose from Methodist sources originally. There are shades or degrees of perfection which are held by these churches. However, all maintain that holiness or sanctification purges the heart of inbred or original sin. Holiness is a distinct experience separate and subsequent to justification or forgiveness, hence the term of the 'second blessing,' which is an instantaneous blessing. It is the crown of Christian experience, visible in charismata of glossalalia, visions, divine revelations, or other forms of 'spirit-baptisms.'

- **The Holiness Church**, also known as the Free Methodist Church, began its work in Egypt in 1902 under the leadership of the Reverend H. I. Randel, later assisted by Bishop Trotter and the Reverend Moore. From 1935–1950 Bishop Black was the outstanding missionary of this denomination. This church has ninety-one congregations and seventy-eight ordained pastors. The church membership is 4,250. The church maintains a Theological College in Asyut. Emphasis is on educational work in under-schooled areas, as well as spiritual renewal and the opening of churches and preaching centers. In 1959, sponsorship of this denomination was transferred from the Canadian Holiness Church to the Free Methodist Church.
- **The Church of Faith in Egypt** has its origin in the missionary endeavors of Louis Glenn and his wife, who in 1905 had settled in Damanhur, later in the Fayyum, and then in Sohag. The work in Upper Egypt, in Sohag and Girga, was supervised by two American ladies, Miss Holdman and Mrs. Jackson. They founded a Bible school in Girga. There is another Bible school in Midan Victoria, Shubra, Cairo. The denomination has nineteen churches, four of which are in Cairo. The others are in Alexandria, Kafr al-Dawar, Abu'l-Matameer, Sohag, Girga, Hawawish, Kom Budar, East Zuq, West Zuq, al-Lahaiwah, Bandar, Abu Shusha, and Girgaris.
- **The Church of God** (Anderson, Indiana) originated in 1880 when a group led by Daniel S. Warner seceded from the Church of God in North America. The issue was that sanctification was seen as a distinctive grace subsequent to justification and the belief in the Parousia of Christ. The church practices baptism by immersion and rejects glossalalia. The first resident Church of God missionary was the Reverend E.A. Reardon, who came to Egypt in 1907, and spent most of his time in Asyut and Alexandria. When Reardon returned to the USA in 1908, he left the mission work in the hands of G.K. Ouzounian, an Armenian minister. Except for short periods of evangelistic work by F.G. Smith in 1913 and H.M. Riggle in 1921, Ouzounian carried on the burden of the work until the arrival of the Reverend Thaddeus Neff in 1923. Under Neff's direction, the mission began to spread to Minya and the Fayyum. The church

maintains sixteen preaching centers with a membership of around a thousand in Cairo, Alexandria, Kafr al-Dawar, Asyut, Minya, Mallawi, Fayyum, Ashmunain, Zueda, New Hadra (Alexandria), Kafr al-Shurafa, and al-Marg. They operate two youth centers in Cairo (St. Andrew's United Church) and in Alexandria.

+ **The Church of the Ideal or the Church of the Standard** was formed in 1920 by a group of Canadian Holiness Movement missionaries. This denomination has about twenty-three congregations in Egypt. The main office for the denomination is in Shubra

The Baptist Evangelical Church was founded in Egypt in 1955 by the Reverend Sadik Wassali Girgis, who began his work in the Fayyum, from where it spread to other parts of the country. The church center is at 271, Shubra Street, Cairo. This denomination, which is supported by the Southern Baptists (United States) has five congregations in Egypt: two in Cairo; one each in Alexandria, Sanuris, Fayyum, and Beni Suef.

The First Baptist Biblical Church was founded by the Reverend Labib Michael in 1961. This denomination has three congregations, two in Cairo, and one in Alexandria.

The Plymouth Brethren were founded by J.N. Darby (1800–1882) in Plymouth. Following several divisions of the movement, the Plymouth, or Exclusive Brethren, refused to take Communion with other Brethren groups. They question infant baptism, celebrate the Lord's Supper weekly, and hold that the official ministry of the Presbyterian churches denies the priesthood of all believers. The beginnings of the Plymouth Brethren in Egypt are associated with the work of the former Presbyterian minister B. Pinkerton, who separated from his church in 1869. Following his return to Egypt in 1874, churches were started in Nakhila, Asyut, Mallawi, Ashmunain, Tahta, Geziret Badran, and Cairo.

The School of Light is owned by the Church of the Brethren and situated on Abu Sinan Street, the main street of Tema, about forty kilometers south of Asyut. The orphanage-school was begun in 1934 by English missionaries. From 1939 to 1959, during which period the school was known as Bethel School, the institution was maintained by a Dutch mission. The school now has seven hundred students. The 'soul' of the school has been Heleen Voorhoeve for many decades.

The Open Brethren or the Church of the Brethren had their beginnings in Schweizenau, Westphalia, Germany in 1708. They are a pietist movement with the New Testament as a "Rule of Faith and Practice." They are pacifists, and follow the dictates of temperance, the simple life, and avoid all luxury. Correct living is more important than certain forms. Baptism is by triune immersion. The footwashing follows John 13:1–17. The Open Brethren were founded in Egypt by Mr. Clapham in 1935. Open Brethren lay stress upon adult baptism and personal witness.

Both 'Open' and 'Closed' Brethren Churches are represented in the total community which numbers about fifteen thousand, grouped in some 165 churches and meeting-places.

The Pentecostal Churches place distinctive emphasis upon sanctification as a separate work of grace, and the climatic experience which is the outpouring of divine gifts, especially also glossalalia (Acts 2:1–4). The Pentecostal experience is held to be the crowning attestation of salvation.

- **The Pentecostal Church or the Apostolic Church** was founded in 1914 by H.I. Randel in cooperation with C.W. Doney and A.H. Post. Their characteristics are baptism of the Holy Spirit and glossalalia, divine healing, and adult baptism. This community of about ten thousand souls is distributed over some 134 churches and meeting-places, which are divided into four districts. By far the most widely known single program related to this denomination is the Asyut Orphanage, now nationally administered and registered with and assisted by the Ministry of Social Affairs, but established in 1911 by Lillian Trasher, then a missionary with the Assemblies of God. The orphanage, formerly known as Lillian Trasher's Orphanage, is situated on the east bank of the Nile opposite Asyut. The orphanage consists of thirteen brick buildings, a church, and a swimming pool. The boys' dormitory covers an area of half an acre. About eight hundred children enjoy boarding and education in the orphanage. In 1911, at the age of twenty-three, Lillian Trasher, inspired by the work of Miss Marker's Faith

Orphanage in North Carolina, sailed for Egypt. Here she was to assist in the Reverend Dunning's Asyut Mission. The direction of her work, however, was determined when a dying Egyptian woman holding her infant in her arms approached her with the request to accept the child. This child was the first orphan of the now famous Asyut Orphanage. At the time of Trasher's death, December 17, 1961, the orphanage in Asyut had an enrollment of 1,300 to whom she was 'Mama Lillian, Godmother of Egypt.' During the fifty years of her service, about eight thousand children passed through her orphanage, which is considered one of the most outstanding welfare institutions of Egypt.[84]

- **The Pentecostal Grace Church or the Church of the Apostolic Blessing** was founded by a Canadian missionary in 1935 at Minya. Their doctrines are similar to those of the Pentecostal Church.
- **The Day of Pentecost Church** with its offices at 10 Fuad Street, Shubra, has not yet been recognized by the Protestant Maglis al-Milli, the Protestant Community Council.
- **The Church of Apostolic Grace** separated from the Pentecostal Grace Church in 1940.
- **The Church of Christ** grew out of the Pentecostal Church in 1948 under the leadership of the Reverend Sami Labib.

The Seventh Day Adventists were founded in 1840 by Ellen G. Harmon-White of Portland, Maine as a millennialist movement, believing in the divinity of Christ, the Trinity, and in the radical observance of the Decalogue. Sabbath observance is essential to the belief in the Parousia and the final judgment. They follow strict temperance, since the body is the Temple of the Holy Spirit (1 Corinthians 6:19). They practice baptism by immersion and foot-washing prior to the Lord's Supper. In 1899 the Irish missionary George Keough began work in Akhmim and Bani Adi, Asyut, and later in Matariya. Their work is largely among Coptic Evangelicals. The Seventh Day Adventist Coptic Denomination was officially registered with the Ministry of the Interior in 1960. They have seventeen active parishes in Lower and Upper Egypt with seven hundred members. The Adventists are not members of the

Protestant Maglis al-Milli. In December 1999, a small group called 'The Keepers of God's Commandments' separated from the main body of Adventists.[85]

The Protestant Community Council (Maglis al-Milli)

The first *waqil* (deputy or representative) of the Evangelical community in Egypt was Girgis Bey Barsum. He was appointed by khedival decree (Ismail Pasha) on June 4, 1878. He enjoyed an important standing with the Sublime Porte. He had deputies in Cairo, Alexandria, Mansura, and Asyut. His successors for more than half a century were all members of the famous Protestant Wissa family of Asyut. Dr. Akhnoukh Fanus (1902–1911) had married Balsam Wissa; Alexan Abiskhirun Pasha (1911–1949) was married to Farouza Wissa; and Alfred Bey Wissa (1950–1956) was the son of Gindy Wissa. With the appointment of the Revered Dr. Ibrahim Said of the Qasr al-Doubara Evangelical Church (1957–1970) the leadership of the Evangelical Community Council was transferred into clerical hands. From 1970–1980 the Reverend Elias Maqar, and from 1980–1997 the Reverend Dr. Samuel Habib represented the Protestant churches. Since 1997 the Reverend Dr. Safwat al-Bayyadi has headed the council with its offices in the Ramses Girls College, Ramses Street.

The Protestant Community council consists of fourteen Protestant churches, which are divided into three groups: the churches of the Reformation; the churches of the Brethren; and the Pentecostal churches. The council consists of twenty members: twelve members represent the Coptic Evangelical Church; six members the other fourteen churches; and two members are women.

Theological Differences between the Coptic Orthodox Church and the Coptic Evangelical Churches

Following an invitation by Pope Shenuda III, the Coptic Evangelical Community Council met on November 1, 1988 with Coptic Orthodox theologians to prepare a theological dialogue between the two churches. Prior to this meeting, conferences with the two churches had taken place in conjunction with the Middle East Council of Churches (MECC) and the Association of Theological Education in the Middle East (ATiME).

Following a discussion about theological agreements based upon the Apostles Creed, the doctrines of the Holy Trinity, incarnation, redemption, resurrection, the Second Coming, and the communion of saints, the issues of disagreement were listed.

These are, for the Coptic Evangelicals: the seven sacraments; the adherence to tradition; the veneration of saints; the hierarchical structure of the church; the laws of fasting and abstinence; and issues pertaining to eschatology.[86]

The first meeting, on January 16, 1989, was held under the joint chairmanship of Pope Shenuda III and the Reverend Dr. Samuel Habib, President of the Coptic Evangelical Church. Further consultations took place on June 27, 1989 and on February 12, 1990.

Agreement was reached about the Sacrament of Baptism, administered in the name of the Holy Trinity. Both churches offer baptism for children upon request of the parents and for adults upon personal confession of faith. Both churches baptize by immersion, while the Coptic Evangelicals also baptize through sprinkling.[87]

However, the main issue between the two Christian communions pertains to their different understanding of the ministry. Because of the sacramental nature of the Coptic Orthodox ministry, the priest offers in the Eucharist a bloodless sacrifice upon the specially consecrated altar. He stands in the apostolic succession of his church which traces its origin to the evangelist St. Mark.[88] For the Coptic Orthodox church only clergymen who are in possession of the apostolic succession are fully accepted as equals. These include those of the various Byzantine orthodox, Oriental orthodox, Roman Catholic, and Episcopal churches. The pastors of the Coptic Evangelical churches do not possess the apostolic succession as interpreted by the orthodox churches.

While the Coptic Orthodox church holds to seven sacraments which are instituted either by Christ or the Apostles,[89] the Coptic Evangelicals practice the sacraments or rites of baptism and the Lord's Supper. Holy matrimony is considered by some Evangelicals as "an order of creation" (Genesis 2:18). For Coptic Orthodox believers, the sacrament of the altar, the Holy Eucharist, is "the divine nourishment by the very Body and Blood of Jesus Christ." On the other hand, Coptic Evangelical Christians of the Reformed or Free-church traditions celebrate the Lord's Supper "in remembrance of Christ" (1 Corinthians 11:24).

The religious authority of the Orthodox Copts are the Canon of Holy Scripture, the canons of the three ecumenical councils of Nicea (325), Constantinople (381), and Ephesus (431), the canons of the fourth- and fifth-century synods, as well as the canons of the pre-Chalcedonian doctors and the medieval canons of Christodoulos, Cyril II and Cyril III.[90] For the Coptic Evangelical Christians, their authorities are the canon of Holy Scripture without the Apocrypha, and in some instances certain confessional statements as to church administration and discipline issued by the respective denomination. Like Coptic Orthodox Christians, Coptic Evangelicals are biblical fundamentalists with a strong tendency toward a literal interpretation of the Bible. Both Western historical and biblical criticism are largely rejected, since one of the worst sins is scepticism, theological error, and biblical unbelief.

The Coptic Orthodox Church is a hierarchical ecclesiastical institution of which the head is the Pope and Patriarch. The Holy Synod consists of all bishops and two clerical representatives of Alexandria and Cairo. The Holy Synod meets at least once a year on the eve of Pentecost. There are metropolitans or archbishops, diocesan bishops, monastic bishops or abbots, and general bishops in charge of certain functions. Parish priests are assisted by deacons, readers, cantors, and subdeacons. The church is systematically clericalized. In sharp contrast to the Coptic Orthodox church, the Coptic Evangelical churches are democratically organized. The Moderator of the Presbyterian Synod of the Nile, as well as those of the eight presbyteries, are elected every year, while the secretaries and treasurers are elected every four years. The electorate consists of 50 percent laity, including women, and 50 percent clergy.

The Coptic Orthodox Church has clearly defined doctrines pertaining to the Holy Virgin as Mother of God. The fifteenth-century Reformation fathers, Martin Luther, Jean Calvin, and Huldrych Zwingli maintained the traditional biblical view of Mary as the Mother of God who retained her virginity *ante partum, in partue*, and *post partum*. Calvin used to call the Holy Virgin the "Mirror of Faith," the example of obedience and trust, while Zwingli stressed the purity of the Holy Virgin. Luther retained the first part of the Ave Maria as praise and glory for the Mother of God. He delivered more than sixty sermons praising the Holy Virgin. The Coptic Evangelical churches practice no particular veneration of the Holy Virgin beyond the references in the New Testament.

Whereas the Coptic Orthodox church venerates 460 saints in the Synaxar,[91] the Evangelical Copts regard some biblical persons as examples for the Christian life to be honored. Evangelical Copts denounce the veneration of icons and relics. In fact, following the iconoclasm of the Coptic Pope Cyril IV, known as the Reformer,[92] the Coptic Evangelical notable Hanna Buqtur Wissa (1837–1907) burnt the icons in the Coptic Orthodox Church in Asyut in 1870.[93]

The Coptic Evangelical churches are non-liturgical in their devotional life and apart from Christmas and Easter some do not celebrate any other Christian feasts. Several of the Coptic Evangelical communities, notably the Brethren, do not even accept any form of Christian symbolism, the cross, or liturgical colors.

While the Coptic Evangelical Christians do not accept the ascetic practices of the Orthodox Copts, fasting, vigils, renunciation, abstinence from certain foods, virginity, temporary continence, silence, and the discipline of mind and wills as means for overcoming the impulse to sin by mortification and self-denial, certain Evangelical Copts—especially the Holiness and Reformed groups—adhere to a strict Calvinistic ethic and regard the body as the temple of the Holy Spirit (1 Corinthians 6:19), therefore demanding strict temperance, abstinence from alcohol, tobacco, and sometimes coffee. For the Lord's Supper, some Coptic Evangelicals use grape juice instead of the biblical wine, which gladdens the heart of man (Psalms 104:15).

4

Christian Agencies, Social and Ecumenical Organizations

The Bible Society of Egypt

The Bible Society in Egypt is a Joint Agency of the British and Foreign Bible Society (BFBS) and the American Bible Society (ABS). The BFBS was founded in London in 1804, whereas the ABS was founded in New York in 1816.

The work of the BFBS in Egypt began in 1818, when William Jowett was sent on a special mission by the Church Missionary Society (CMS) to collect information as to the state of religion in Egypt, and to discover the best methods for the propagation of Christian knowledge. Jowett went as far as Edfu and Aswan, where he visited many Coptic churches and monasteries. Also in 1818, Christopher Burckhart, a young companion of Jowett, obtained from the Coptic Patriarch the permission to serve as a representative of the BFBS in the distribution of Holy Scriptures.

The work of the ABS in Egypt began in 1836 with the arrival of S.H. Calhoun, who was their first agent to work in the Middle East. He was one of the 251 missionaries sent by the ABS between the years 1820 and 1861.

After the opening of the Suez Canal in 1869, the Society tried to develop work in Egypt more systematically. A full-time worker was sent to Alexandria in 1870, and limited colportage was undertaken. In 1883, shortly after the British occupation, Egypt was made a separate BFBS agency, which also covered Syria, Palestine, the Sudan, Ethiopia, and East Africa. Colportage was developed at Alexandria, Cairo, Upper Egypt, and among the ships at Port Said.

In 1902–1903 negotiations with the ABS and American Missions produced an agreement that the BFBS should work in the Delta and Lower Egypt and the ABS in Upper Egypt, with Cairo and Alexandria as common ground. In 1937 a joint agency with the ABS was set up, administered by the BFBS until the Suez crisis of 1956 when the ABS took over at short notice. In 1963 the first Egyptian general Secretary was appointed, the Reverend Dr. Abdel-Masih Istafanous, and he began to develop work with and through the churches rather than by employing colporters. The Bible Society in Egypt was inaugurated in 1966 and became an associate member of the United Bible Societies (UBS) in 1977. Ramez Atallah, the present General Secretary, took over the leadership in 1990.

The first Bible Society Bookshop was established in Alexandria in 1883. In 1937, the Cairo Bookshop at 74 al-Gumhuriya Street was opened. Further bookshops exist in Tanta and Port Said. In 1999, two bookshops were opened in Minya and Asyut, and in 2000 two additional shops were established in Luxor and Mansura.

The first Arabic printed Bibles were the Arabic versions of the Paris and London Polyglots (Hebraica, Samaritana, Chaldaica, Graeca, Syriaca, Latina, Arabica, Paris 1629–1645). The *Congregatio de Propaganda fide* published a Biblia Sacra Arabica in three volumes in 1671, which was followed by the Smith-Van Dyck version of 1865. In 1876 and 1878, the Jesuit version *Al-kitab al-muqaddas* was published in Beirut. Both the Smith-Van Dyck and the Jesuit versions are used by the Copts. The former is more widely distributed and, therefore, more widely read by the Egyptians. Whereas the Jesuit version is admired by the learned, the Smith-van Dyck version is more understandable for the average reader.

The Young Men's Christian Association in Egypt

The YMCA was founded in England in 1844 by George Williams (1821–1905), to promote social and religious work among young men. It grew out of meetings for prayer and Bible-reading, which Williams held among his fellow-workers in a dry-goods business in London. Similar associations had been founded earlier in Scotland. The movement spread rapidly; in 1852, the YMCA was organized in the USA and in Canada. In 1891, the first foreign work was organized in India by the American YMCA.

In 1896, the first College YMCA was begun in Asyut as a result of a visit of Dr. John R. Mott. In February 1909, efforts were made to organize a Cairo Association of the YMCA. An Arabic branch was established in 1910, followed by the Anglo-American Branch in 1920. In 1921, the YMCA was organized in Alexandria, and in 1922 in Asyut. In January 1923, the

Central Branch at al-Gumhuriya Street was opened to Egyptians. A staff of six trained secretaries, five from the United States and one from England, were appointed to Egypt. In 1923, the International Committee of the YMCA purchased two acres of land in Cairo, the site of a large palace belonging to a former Prime Minister. The building was converted into a well-equipped YMCA center. In 1930, the famous Pont Limun Club for needy boys was organized.

The Federation of the YMCA in Egypt has the following local associations which are situated in: Cairo, Alexandria, Asyut, Minya, Sohag, Abu Qurqas, Quweisna, Port Said, and Luxor. The YMCA in Egypt has not only been instrumental in leadership training throughout Egypt, it has helped to start the movement in Ethiopia and in several other Middle Eastern countries.

The Young Women's Christian Association in Egypt

The YWCA was founded in 1855 by two ladies simultaneously. In the south of England Miss Emma Roberts started a prayer union with a purely spiritual aim, and in London Lady Kinnaird commenced the practical work by opening homes and institutes for young women in business. In 1887, the two branches united in the YWCA, which seeks to promote the welfare of young women through holiday homes, clubs, and resthouses as well as classes and lectures.

The National Association of the YWCA in Egypt has four local associations. The Cairo Association is situated at 11 'Imad al-Din Street with the hostel at 4 Naus Bey Street, Antikhana, and the center at 17, Midan Qubbat al-Hawa, Shubra, and Pyramids Camp. The Alexandria Association is situated at 66 Nabi Daniel Street. The Minya Association has its offices in YWCA Hall, and the Asyut Association is situated at Naguib Qaldas Street.

The first YWCA hostel in Egypt was established in 1902. Today, this hostel serves eighty women and girls. In 1918, a professional school for languages, shorthand and secretarial training was established. The first holiday camp was inaugurated in 1923, and by 1961 over seven hundred campers have benefited by the programs offered at Sidi Bishr, Alexandria, and Mandara. The Pyramids' Desert Camp was built in 1928 for the purpose of bringing women together for study and recreation. The National Girls Movement, the Blue Triangle Girls, was formed in 1933. At present there are eight groups of Blue Triangle Girls. A luncheon service for shop assistants and secretaries was inaugurated in 1951.

The Social Organizations

BLESS: The Bishopric of Public, Ecumenical and Social Services of the Coptic Orthodox Church, Development Department (DD)

The Coptic Orthodox Program for Ecumenical and Social Services was founded by Pope Cyril VI (1959–1971). On September 30, 1962 he consecrated Father Makari al-Suriani (Sa'ad Aziz) as General Bishop Samuel for Social, Ecumenical and Public Affairs, an office which he held until his assassination on October 6, 1981. In 1954, Pope Yusab II had delegated Father Makari to represent the Coptic Orthodox church at the Second World Council of Churches Assembly at Evanston, Illinois. A year later he received his master's degree from Princeton University. Engaged in ecumenical and in social projects, urban and rural, Bishop Samuel became the initiator of BLESS. He had the full confidence of Pope Cyril VI and represented the Coptic Orthodox church in ecumenical, political, and social gatherings. He laid down the organizational foundation for the national and international work of the new bishopric. As head of the Social Studies Department in the Coptic Institute he had all the resources at his disposal to create a successful and effective Christian agency. Following his death, the bishopric was directed by Bishop Serapion until Pope Shenuda consecrated him on November 14, 1995 as bishop of Los Angeles, USA. Since then the bishopric is directed by Bishop Yo'annis, secretary of H.H. Pope Shenuda.

The purpose of BLESS-DD is "to discover and develop peoples' potentials in order to meet their community needs for an abundant life for all." Therefore, "to empower people to effectively participate in development processes, networking with GOs and NGOs . . . to enable women in target communities to participate effectively . . . with awareness toward children's rights. . . ."

BLESS-DD engages in primary health care, through education, home visits, seminars, vaccination campaigns, nutrition classes, poly- and mobile clinics, care for pregnant women, combatting female genital mutilation, constructing pit latrines, and providing potable water.

The economic program includes agricultural and centenarian services, pilot cultivation models, women cottage industries, loans for small projects, networking with businessmen for employment, literacy classes, and teacher training.

The child program specializes in developing modern nursing facilities, clubs for children aged six through twelve years, skill development and social activities, and training courses in bible studies.

The Center for Human Resource Development (CCHRD), the Center for Social Studies (CCSS), and the Center for Public Relations (CCPR) are integral parts of BLESS-DD. They offer training courses for staff members inside and outside of Egypt, and they assist in communication through the various news media. They also advocate changing the attitudes of the Copts toward civil society issues.

In 1998 BLESS-DD started its Comprehensive Integral Development (CID) in seven communities. Today twenty-nine communities are served by BLESS-DD-CID.

Upper Egypt

Aswan Diocese: Daraw village, Redisia village.
Qus Diocese: al-Ayaysha village
Deshna Diocese: al-Rahmania village
Nag' Hammadi Diocese: al-Marashda village
Balyana Diocese: Dair al-Naganish village
Girga Diocese: Nag' al-Qasria village
Akhmim Diocese: al-Hawawish village
Sohag Diocese: al-Wastania village

Middle Egypt

Tahta Diocese: Nag' al-Sik village
Tema Diocese: Nag' al-Suq village
Abu Tig Diocese: Dewena village
Manfalut Diocese: al-Gawley village
Abnub Diocese: Dair al-Gabrawi village
Al-Qusiya Diocese: Ezbet al-Usquf village
Asyut Diocese: al-Mahmudia village
Dair Mawas Diocese: Nazlet Abdel Masih village
Malawi Diocese: Dair al-Malak village

Cairo and Beni Suef

Beni Suef Diocese: al-Dair Wazaiet village,
Dair al-Maimun village
Maadi Diocese: Ezbet al-Nasr area
Old Cairo: Ezbet Kheirallah area

Lower Egypt

Shibin al-Qanatir Diocese: Hud al-Henna area
Al-Qalubia Diocese: al-Safra village
Benha Diocese: Ezbet al-Kassis and Kafr al-Nasara village
Sharqia Diocese: Kafr Awad Suliman village
Behaira Diocese: Abu Hamra and Labib Suliman villages.

Caritas–Egypt

The foundation of Caritas–Internationalis was initiated by the State Secretariat of the Holy See in Holy Week, September 1950. Prior to to this, European relief organizations were already collaborating on an international level under the name of "Caritas Catholica," thereafter known as "Caritas Internationalis." Today, there are 154 Caritas organizations in 198 countries and territories on five continents. Of these, sixteen are in the Arab world.

After the Arab-Israeli conflict in June 1967, Caritas–Egypt was established to take care of the refugees and displaced persons from the Suez Canal Zone. Caritas–Egypt now has 1,300 employees with half a million beneficiaries a year. Caritas has paid special attention to the medico-social centers since its foundation in 1967. These include mother and child protection services, literacy classes for women, sewing classes, model kindergartens, care for the mentally handicapped, cultural excursions, social aid grants to the poorest and a service for the urban street children, preventing them from becoming delinquents.

The medico-social centers are in Matariya (1976), Bulaq (1970), Haggana on the Suez road (1988), Kafr al-Sisi (1971), Umraniya (1974), Abu Zaabel (1984) and al-Ayat (1994). In 2002, 105,624 persons were served at these centers, 203 persons attended the literacy classes, and 840 children were enrolled in the kindergartens. The project of giving small loans to execute useful projects for the benefit of the family has been applied in 1,785 projects in villages in the Asyut and Sohag regions. The Caritas literacy program operates from five offices: Alexandria serving the Delta; Minya; Asyut; Sohag; and Luxor covering Upper Egypt, including Qena and Aswan. In this program Caritas works with UNICEF and other governmental and non-governmental agencies.

Since 1976 Caritas has taken care of African and Asian refugees, and elderly stateless persons, by offering monthly allowances, scholarships, medical care, marriage expenses, and kindergarten facilities. The 'Oasis of Hope' center, situated on the Cairo-Alexandria highway at kilometer seventy-two was established by Caritas–Freiburg, Germany, to provide therapy and rehabilitation for drug addicts. The center is operated by a team of qualified psychiatrists and social workers. The Youth Sector of Caritas provides summer camps, international camps, and a variety of youth activities. This work began in 1978.

Caritas gives special attention to those suffering from Hansen's Disease, working together with the Department of Leprosy Control. Medical examinations of lepers are conducted in the ten governorates. Physiotherapists are employed to work with the lepers; and service-workshops have been set up to manufacture orthopedic shoes and sandals, artificial limbs, prostheses and or theses, at Abu Zaabel. Since its foundation in 1982, the SETI center seeks to find solutions to the problems of the mentally handicapped, to improve their quality of life by making the best use of the available resources. In 1988 the Psychic Health Program was initiated to provide assistance at the Khanka Hospital. The general Health Sector programs (1986) are to further 'health awareness,' including the treatment of malnutrition cases, especially among children in Upper Egypt.

The Association of Upper Egypt for Education and Development

The Association of Upper Egypt for Education and Development (AUEED) was established in Upper Egypt in 1940, when the Jesuit fathers founded it and appointed Father Henry Ayrout, s.j. (1908–1969), to manage it. The AUEED projects were financially supported by several wealthy Egyptian families, and AUEED provided its tuition-free education before the government initiated this program on a national level. The general assembly members decided once in 1971 and again in 1990 to change the name from 'The Catholic Association for Schools in Egypt' to be 'The Association of Upper Egypt for Education and Development.' In 1960, the AUEED constructed a center for empowering women in Akhmim, offering vocational training. To this day, the products of this center have earned a worldwide reputation through the annual exhibitions in Cairo.

The AUEED established four offices in Upper Egypt for managing the activities in Minya (1982), Asyut (1985), Sohag (1992), and Luxor (1998). It owns thirty-six primary schools with a capacity for 10,500 girls and boys, both Christians and Muslims. In addition, the association has sixty-three development centers providing for health, youth, women, and vocational training programs, according to the community needs. The majority of the students belong to low socioeconomic levels whose parents are agricultural laborers *(fellahin)* with no land ownership, or a limited ownership of two feddans or less.[94]

Gender awareness is a cross-cutting dimension in the entire program of AUEED. It aims at empowering women in the traditionally patriarchal communities. The gender project implemented in thirteen villages in Asyut and eight villages in Sohag lays stress on issues of gender discrimination. The ultimate goal of the Association's Women Empowerment Program (WEP) is to facilitate the process for women to assume their vital role in both family and society on an equal footing with men. Female circumcision is a firmly entrenched tradition (98.4 percent are circumcised). In thirty-four centers in Minya, Asyut, Sohag, and Luxor the WEP has served 3,400 women and 1,350 young girls so far. In the center in Bayadiya, Minya, not a single incidence of female circumcision has been registered in the past five years.

All over Upper Egypt, the association maintains twenty-seven Mother and Child Health Care Centers. It provides medical services for people with diabetes free of charge.

In Asyut the AUEED maintains an ophthalmological clinic in Zarabi, an ophthamological and dermatological clinic in Dair al-Ganadla, and another clinic in Abu Qurqas. More than thirty-six thousand benefit from these dispensaries and clinics annually.

The illiteracy rate in Upper Egypt is 43.9 percent of the total Egyptian population, with the women's rate being 68 percent, the main reason for AUEED. The association's founder, Reverend Father Henry H. Ayrout, wrote his Ph.D. dissertation entitled "Customs and Habits of the Peasant" at the University of Lyons, completing it in 1938, which he published later as *The Egyptian Peasant.*[95] The book provided the basis for the methodology and aims of the AUEED.

The Coptic Evangelical Organization for Social Services

The founder of the Coptic Evangelical Organization for Social Services (CEOSS), the Reverend Dr. Samuel Habib, experienced at first hand the desperate conditions of the Egyptian *fellahin* as a young man of twenty-two years of age, when he spent five months in the small Upper Egyptian village Herz in the district of Minya. At this time he was engaged in the recently established literacy program (the Lit-Lit methodology of Frank Laubach) designed to teach the Egyptian villagers to read and to write. He was profoundly touched by the crushing poverty and the deplorable living conditions which he witnessed there. It was this crucial experience that laid the foundation for CEOSS as a movement to relieve the injustices, the innocent sufferings, and the hopeless misery of his countrymen.

CEOSS, a Protestant civil non-profit organization with roots in the Evangelical Presbyterian Synod of the Nile, had its beginnings in 1950. Ten years later, CEOSS was registered with the Ministry of Social Affairs. Reformed theological concepts (based upon Max Weber) and practical scientific experiences have framed its programs. The purpose of CEOSS is to improve the quality of life in impoverished communities in the fields of health, education, economics, agriculture, and environment preservation. CEOSS offers credit and supportive services to the entrepreneurial poor, especially destitute women, and to establish income generating projects.

CEOSS builds up the abilities of poor and marginalized communities and individuals to effect change so that they can live dignified lives. CEOSS encourages mobilization of local resources, partnerships with multiple stakeholders, and networking with concerned organizations to create and have a long-lasting impact.

To promote a culture of dialogue based on pluralistic democratic approaches and respect for human rights, CEOSS invites Christian and Muslim religious leaders, intellectuals, and media opinion-makers to study contemporary social issues objectively, analytically, and cordially, thereby building mutual understanding and trust. Through dialogue and cooperative learning, CEOSS encourages people to work together to promote reconciliation, peace, and progress. CEOSS promotes enlightened thought in the reformed theological perspective to encourage a broadened vision and role for the Egyptian church and Egyptian civil society.

The Ecumenical Organizations

The Middle East Council of Churches

The history of the Middle East Council of Churches (MECC) can be traced to the first ecumenical efforts following the 1910 Edinburgh Missionary Conference when Christians gathered in Jerusalem to form a regional organization. In 1928 the organization became known as the Near East Christian Council (NECC) of missionary societies and encompassed a few indigenous evangelical churches from Morocco to Iran, and from Turkey to the Sudan. In 1964, the NECC changed its name to the Near East Council of Churches. Ten years later, the NECC gave way to a Middle East Council of Churches with the inclusion of the Oriental (non-Chalcedonian) and Byzantine (Chalcedonian) churches, thereby reflecting the richness and diversity of the Middle East. In 1990, at the Fifth General Assembly of the MECC, the seven Catholic churches of the Middle East joined the council.

The members of the MECC adhere to the historical confessions of the early church, the Apostles' and Nicene Creeds. Larger and smaller families each have equal voice in the deliberations of the council. The decision-making body is the Council's General Assembly of ninety-six members representing the four ecclesiastical families. They meet every four years. For the interim period, an executive committee with a general secretary carries on with the daily work.

The member churches of the MECC are organized into four families.

The Oriental (non-Chalcedonian) Orthodox Churches:

The Coptic Orthodox Church
The Armenian Apostolic Church
The Armenian Catholicosate of Cilicia
The Syrian Orthodox Church of Antioch

The Eastern (Chalcedonian) Orthodox Churches:

The Greek Orthodox Church of Alexandria
The Greek Orthodox Church of Antioch
The Greek Orthodox Church of Jerusalem
The Orthodox Church of Cyprus

The Catholic Churches:

The Maronite Church of Antioch
The Greek Catholic Melkite Church of Antioch, Alexandria and Jerusalem
The Armenian Catholic Church
The Syrian Catholic Church of Antioch
The Coptic Catholic Church
The Latin Patriarchate of Jerusalem
The Chaldean Catholic Church

The Evangelical Churches

The Coptic Evangelical Synod of the Nile
The Union of Armenian Evangelical Churches
The National Evangelical Synod of Syria and the Lebanon
National Evangelical Union of Lebanon
The Episcopal Church in Jerusalem and the Middle East
The Evangelical Lutheran Church of Jordan
The National Evangelical Church in Kuwait
The Evangelical Churches in Iran, Algeria, Tunisia, and the Sudan

The Oriental (Non-Chalcedonian) Orthodox Churches in the Middle East

"Throughout history, we lived a concrete unity in faith, theology and doctrines. We experienced our oneness through the first Ecumenical Councils of Nicea 325, Constantinople 381, and Ephesus 431. We continue to live our unity of faith through church life, and interchurch and ecumenical relations."

The presidents are: H.H. Pope Shenuda III of Alexandria and Patriarch of the See of St. Mark; H.H. Patriarch Mar Ignatius Zakka I of Antioch and all the East; H.H. Catholicos Aram I of the Great House of Cilicia of the Armenian Orthodox Church.

Other members belonging to the Oriental Orthodox family are the Ethiopian Orthodox Tewahedo Church, the Eritrean Orthodox Church, and the Malankara Orthodox Syrian Church.

5
Christian Feasts and Fasts

The Coptic Orthodox Calendar of Feasts and Fasts

The dates for the feasts and fasts of Easter/Pentecost depend upon the movable Easter dates. The number of fasting days are in parentheses.

*	January 7	Feast of the Nativity of Christ[1]
†	January 14	Circumcision of Christ
§	January 18	Vigil of the Feast of Christ's Baptism (1)
*	January 19	Manifestation of Christ's Divinity (Epiphany)
†	January 21	Christ's First Miracle at Cana
‡	January 29	Dormition of the Virgin Mary
†	February 15	Presentation of Christ in the Temple
	March 19	Invention of the Holy Cross
‡	April 2	Apparition of the Virgin Mary at Zeitun in 1968
‡	May 9	Nativity of the Virgin Mary
§	May 31	Beginning Fast for the Holy Apostles (42)
†	June 1	Entrance of Christ into Egypt
	July 12	Feast of the Holy Apostles
§	August 7	Beginning Fast of the Holy Virgin Mary (15)
†	August 19	Transfiguration of Christ
‡	August 22	Assumption of the Virgin Mary
	September 11	New Year's Day *(Niruz)*
§	November 26	Beginning Fast for the Nativity of Christ (42)
‡	December 12	Presentation of the Virgin Mary in the Temple

1. The Coptic Christmas is the only Christian holiday recognized as an Egyptian national holiday.

The movable feasts are:

§	Great Lent	(55)
*	Palm Sunday	Entrance of Christ in Jerusalem
†	Holy Thursday	Institution of the Lord's Supper
*	Easter	Feast of the Resurrection of Christ
*	Ascension	Christ's Ascension in Heaven
*	Pentecost	The Descent of the Holy Spirit

Key

* * The Major Feasts of Our Lord
* † The Minor Feasts of Our Lord
* ‡ The Feasts of the Holy Virgin Mary
* § Fasts

The Major Greek Orthodox Feasts

In addition to Sundays, the following are the Major Greek Orthodox Feasts:

January 1	Circumcision of Our Lord and Feast of St. Basil
January 6	Epiphany
January 7	Feast of St. John the Baptist
January 30	Feast of the Three Hierarchs (SS. Basil the Great, John Chrysostom, Gregory the Theologian)
February 2	Presentation of Our Lord
March 25	Annunciation
April 23	Feast of St. George
	Easter Monday*
May 21	Feast of SS. Constantine and Helena
	Ascension*
	Whit Monday*
June 24	Nativity of St. John the Baptist
June 29	Feast of SS. Peter and Paul
June 30	Synaxis of the Twelve Apostles
July 1	Feast of the Unmercenary Saints (SS. Cosmas and Damian)
July 20	Feast of Elijah the Prophet
August 6	Metamorphosis (Transfiguration)
August 15	Dormition of the Holy Virgin Mary
August 29	Decapitation of St. John the Baptist
September 8	Nativity of the Blessed Virgin Mary
September 14	Exaltation of the Holy Cross
October 26	Feast of St. Demetrius

November 1	Second Feast of the Unmercenary Saints
November 8	Feast of St. Michael and All Archangels
November 21	Entry of the Holy Virgin Mary into the Temple
November 25	Feast of St. Catherine
November 30	Feast of St. Andrew
December 4	Feast of St. Barbara
December 5	Feast of St. Sabas
December 6	Feast of St. Nicholas
December 12	Feast of St. Spyridon
December 25	Nativity of Our Lord
December 26	Synaxis of the Holy Virgin Mary
December 27	Feast of St. Stephen

* Moveable feasts

The Major Armenian Orthodox Feasts

In addition to Sundays, the following are the Major Armenian Orthodox Feasts:

January 6	Epiphany (Nativity and Epiphany)
January 13	Circumcision of Our Lord
January 14†	Feast of St. John the Baptist
April 7	Annunciation
May*	Ascension
June*	Dedication of the Cathedral at Echmiadzin
July*	Feast of St. Gregory the Illuminator
August*	Transfiguration of Jesus Christ
August 15†	Assumption of the Virgin
September 8	Nativity of the Virgin
September 14†	Exaltation of the Cross
November 21	Presentation of the Virgin
December 9	Immaculate Conception
December 26	Feast of St. Stephen

† Feast transferred to the following Sunday.
* Moveable feasts.

The Feast of the Transfiguration (Vartavar)

The Feast of the Transfiguration of Jesus Christ, besides being a religious feast, is one which has special national significance for the Armenians. While the Byzantines and the Latins celebrate it on August 6, and the Armenians used to. But this coincided with the day on which was observed the great pagan feast Vartavar was observed. In the course of time, the Armenians began to celebrate the Assumption of the Holy Virgin in August, instead of the Transfiguration of Jesus Christ, which was transferred to the fourteenth week after Easter. Though the Feast of the Transfiguration was separated from the traditional date of Vartavar, the traditional festivities of this ancient feast were retained and attached to the festivities of the Christian feast.

The Feast of the Varaka Cross *(Hripsimiants)*

In AD 300, during the persecution of the first Christians in Armenia by Tirtade I, a group of thirty-seven young virgins (later known as the Hripsimian Virgins) under the leadership of Lady Cayane, left their residence at the Hociats Monastery, after donating a greatly cherished small piece of the Cross to the monks living there. The latter buried this on the side of the Varaka Mountain. The virgins descended the mountain, and settled in a barn at its base. However, they were soon discovered by the king's men, who surrounded the place. One of the virgins named Hripsime was known for her great beauty and kindness. The king, hearing of her, asked her for hand in marriage. Her persistent refusal to marry a pagan enraged him, and he subsequently ordered all the virgins to be put to death. The Feast of the Varaka Cross is unique to the Armenians, and it is celebrated on the first Sunday following September 28.

The Commemoration of the Vartanants and Ghevontiants

In 430, Armenia became subject to the Sassanid dynasty of Persia, and the Armenians had to pay tribute to the Persians and to provide them with soldiers. In 449, Hazgerd II of Persia issued a decree, ordering all his Christian subjects to become fire-worshipers (Zoroastrians). The Armenians sent a letter to the Persian king informing him that nothing would make them change their faith, not even fire, sword, or angels.

The Governor of Armenia, who had been appointed by the Persians, went to the Persian capital together with a group of ministers, princes, and the general Vartan Mamigonian. However, they soon realized that they had fallen into a trap, and feigning acceptance of fire-worship as their new religion, they returned to Armenia in order to save their people from the enemy. However, groups of pagan priests had already been sent to convert the Armenians. Archbishop Ghevont Yerets led the inhabitants of Ankegh against the pagan priests and the latter were thwarted. The entire nation united to prepare for a battle against the Persians. A battle took place near Avarair, where sixty thousand Armenians faced two hundred thousand Persians. The Armenians were defeated, and their commander-in-chief, General Vartan, was killed, together with 1,035 soldiers. The Persians captured nine of the Christian leaders, among them the Catholicus and Archbishop Ghevont Yerets. He is remembered to this day as one of the most eminent religious figures in Armenian history.

Although the Armenians were defeated, it was a great moral victory for them because the enemy failed to make the Christians apostatize, the struggle continued for thirty-three years, resulting in the final defeat of the Persian forces and an agreement was reached by the Treaty of Nvarssak in 485. Thus Vartanants represents one of the most glorious pages in Armenian history. To this day, the Armenian church commemorates the Vartanants every year on the February 21. The martyrdom of the nine religious leaders (Ghevontiants) is commemorated on February 19.

The Commemoration of April 24, 1915

The last Armenian Kingdom in Armenia was destroyed by the Seljuks in 1048, while the last Armenian Kingdom in Cilicia (New Armenia) was brought to an end by the Ottoman Turks in 1375. Armenia was then subjected to Turkish rule. Thus began the darkest and longest eclipse in their history.

The year 1915 represents the greatest tragedy in Armenian history, for the Turkish government under the leadership of Talaat, Enver, and Jemal organized a systematic annihilation of the Armenians. This plan began with the arrest and murder of Armenian intellectuals on the night of April 24, 1915, when around three hundred people were killed in one night. After that, the mass massacre of the nation began. They were driven in the direction of the deserts of Mesopotamia. Under the supervision of armed guards, they were forced to walk for miles night and day. The elderly, children, and pregnant women, who could not continue walking, were flogged to death. All along the way, bands of Turkish soldiers attacked these people continuously.

To this day, Armenians all over the world commemorate the one million Armenians who died in 1915. Every year, on the April 24, the Armenian Church celebrates a Requiem Liturgy for all those who perished during these days of persecution.

The Commemoration of May 28, 1918

In March 1917, following the Russian Revolution, the Kerensky government established a special committee for Transcaucasia. However, early in 1918, Transcaucasia declared itself independent of Russia, and a government was set up in Tiflis titled the Democratic Federal Republic of Transcaucasia. It was made up of Armenians, Georgians, and the Tartars of Azerbaijan. It lasted for five weeks only.

On May 15, the Turkish military attacked, and after a fierce encounter with the Armenians, entered Alexandropol (now Leninakan). The Armenians employed what strength they could muster, and under the command of General Silikian and General Tro counter-attacked the exposed Turkish positions. They fought for five days, from May 23 to May 28, and defeated the Turks. Meanwhile, the federation was renounced, and both Georgia and Azerbaijan declared their independence.

Having expelled the Turkish armies from their country, the Armenians declared their land an independent republic. In great contrast to April 24, 1915, the May 28, 1918, is a glorious and happy day for most Armenians.

The Major Catholic Feasts in Egypt

In addition to Sundays, the following are the major feasts of the various rites of the Catholic Church in Egypt.

			Armenian	Chaldean	Coptic	Melkite	Latin	Maronite	Syrian
January	1	Circumcision of our Lord	x	x	x	x	x	x	x
January	6	Epiphany	°	°	°	°	°	°	°
January	7	Second Day of Epiphany				x			
February	2	Purification of the Virgin	x	x		x			x
February	9	St. Maron						°	
March	9	St. Ephraem							°
March	19	St. Joseph		x			x	x	x
March	25	Annunciation	x	x		°			
April	*	Easter Sunday	x	x		x			x
April	*	Easter Monday				x			
April	23	St. George		x					
May	15	Our Lady of the Fields		x					
May	*	Ascension	°	°	°	°	°	°	°
June	*	Whit Monday				x			
June	*	Corpus Christi		x		x	x	x	x
June	29	SS. Peter and Paul		x	°	x	x	x	x
July	3	St. Thomas			x				
June	*	St. Gregory the Illuminator	°						
August	6	Transfiguration		x		x			
August	15	Assumption of the Virgin	°	°	°	°	°	°	°
August	29	St. Bartholomew			x				
September	8	Nativity of the Virgin	x	x		x	x	x	
September	14	Exaltation of the Cross		x		x		x	
November	1	All Saints			x		°		x
November	21	Presentation of the Virgin				x		x	
December	8	Immaculate Conception		x	x		x		x
December	9	Immaculate Conception	x			x		°	
December	25	Christmas	°	°	°	°	°		°
December	26	Day After Christmas		x		x			
December	27	St. Stephen		x					

* Movable feasts.

° Feasts of obligation according to the 1961 ruling. The Chaldean rite in Egypt observes the Feast of Our Lady of Fatima (October 13) as a Day of Obligation.

The Dates of Easter (Latin and Orthodox), 2007–2020

The Dates of Easter (Latin and Orthodox), 2007–2020

Western or Latin Easter		Eastern or Orthodox Easter
2007	April 8	April 8
2008	March 23	April 27
2009	April 12	April 19
2010	April 4	April 4
2011	April 24	April 24
2012	April 8	April 15
2013	March 31	May 5
2014	April 20	April 20
2015	April 5	April 12
2016	March 27	May 1
2017	April 16	April 16
2018	April 1	April 8
2019	April 21	April 28
2020	April 12	April 19

6

The Hierarchs of the Churches Represented in Egypt

The Chalcedonian Orthodox Hierarchs (19th–21st Centuries)

Greek Orthodox Patriarchs of Alexandria

Parthenios II (1788–1805)
Theophilos II (1805–1825)
Hierotheos I (1825–1845)
Artemios (1845–1847)
Hierotheos II (1847–1858)
Kallinikos (1858–1861)
Jakobos II (1861–1865)
Nikanor (1866–1869)
Sophronios IV (1870–1899)
Photios (1900–1926)
Meletios II (1926–1935)
Nikolaos V (1935–1939)
Christophoros (1939–1967)
Nikolaos VI (1968–1986)
Parthenios III (1987–1996)
Petros VII (1997–2004)
Theodoros II (2004–)
Theodoros II is the 115th successor of St. Mark

The Greek Orthodox Archbishops of St. Catherine, Sinai

Konstantinos (1804–1859)
Kyrillos III (1859–1867)
Kallistratos (1867–1885)
Porphyrios I (1885–1904)

Porphyrios II (1904–1926)
Porphyrios III (1926–1969)
Gregorios II (1969–1973)
Damianos (1973–)

Greek Orthodox Patriarchs of Antioch

Euthymios I (1792–1813)
Seraphim I (1818–1823)
Methodios I (1843–1859)
Hierotheos I (1859–1885)
Gerasimos I (1885–1891)
Spyridon I (1892–1898)
Melethios II (1899–1906)
Gregory IV (1906–1928)
Alexander III (1928–1958)
Theodosius VI (1958–1970)
Elias IV (1970–1979)
Ignatius IV Hazim (1979–)
Ignatius IV is the 170th successor of St. Peter

The Non-Chalcedonian Orthodox Hierarchs (19th–21st Centuries)

Coptic Orthodox Patriarchs of Alexandria

Mark VIII (1796–1809)
Peter VII (1809–1852)
Cyril IV (1854–1861)
Demetrius II (1861–1870)
Cyril V (1874–1926)
John XIX (1928–1942)
Macarius III (1942–1945)
Yasab II (1946–1956)
Cyril VI (1959–1971)
Shenuda III (1971–)
Shenuda III is the 117th successor of St. Mark

Armenian Catholici of St. Echmiadzine and All Armenians

David V (1801–1807)
Daniel (1802–1808)
Yeprem (1809–1830)

John VIII (1831–1842)
Nerses V (1843–1857)
Matthew I (1858–1865)
George IV (1866–1882)
Magar (1885–1891)
Mgrdich (1892–1907)
Matthew II (1908–1910)
George V (1911–1930)
Khoren (1932–1938)
George VI (1945–1954)
Vasken (1955–1994)
Karekin I (1995–1999)
Karekin II (1999–)

Syrian Orthodox Patriarchs of Antioch

Ignatius XXIX Mattai (1780–1817)
Ignatius XXX Jonas (1818–1836)
Ignatius XXXI Georgis V (1818–1836)
Ignatius XXXII Eliyas II (1838–1847)
Ignatius XXXIII Jakob II (1848–1871)
Ignatius XXXIV Petros IV (1872–1891)
Ignatius XXXV Abdulmessiah II (1895–1905)
Ignatius XXXVI Abdallah (1906–1915)
Ignatius XXXVII Eliyas III (1917–1931)
Ignatius XXXVIII Ephrem I (1933–1957)
Ignatius XXXIX Jacob III (1957–1980)
Ignatius XL Zakkai I (1980–)
Zakkai I is the 140th successor of St. Peter

Armenian Catholici of the Great House of Cilicia and the Middle East

Giragos I (1797–1822)
Yeprem II (1822–1833)
Michael II (1833–1855)
Giragos II (1855–1866)
Mekerdich (1871–1894)
Sahag II (1902–1939)
Bedros IV (1940)
Karekin I (1943–1952)
Zareh (1956–1952)

Khoren (1963–1983)
Karekin II (1977–1995)
Aram I (1995–)

The Catholic Hierarchs (19th–21st Centuries)

Coptic Catholic Patriarchs of Alexandria

Cyril Macarius (1895)
Mark Khouzam (1948–1958)
Stephanus I (1958–1986)
Stephanus II Ghattas (1986–)

Maronite Bishops of Cairo

Joseph Darian (1906–1920)
Emmanuel Fares (1928–1943)
Pierre Dib (1947–1965)
Joseph Merhi (1972–1989)
Joseph Dergham (1989–)

Chaldean Catholic Bishops of Cairo

Petros Abad (1890–1912)
Joseph Gharib (1912–1920)
Petros Aziz (1920–1928)
Paul Bero (1928–1932)
Sulaiman Ousta (1932–1939)
Emmanuel Rassam (1939–1964)
Ephraem Bédé (1964–1971)
Thomas Bedawid (1971)
Ephraem Bédé (1971–1984)
Youssef Sarraf (1984–)

Apostolic Vicariate for the Latins in Egypt

Egidio Samperiri (1978–2001)
Joseph Bausardo (2001–)

Greek Melkite Catholic Patriarchs of Alexandria and Antioch

Maximos III Mazlum (1838–1855)
Clemens Bahus (1856–1864)
Gregory II Y. Sayur (1864–1897)
Peter IV Geragiri (1898–1902)
Cyril VIII Geha (1903–1916)
Demetrius I Cadi (1919–1925)

Cyril IX Moghabghab (1928–1947)
Maximos IV Sayegh (1947–1967)
Gregory III Laham (2002–)

Syrian Catholic Bishops of Cairo

Basil Kandalaft (1895–1904)
Ignac Nouri (1904–1913)
Raphael Gibri (1914–1925)
Julian B. Kalian (1925–1928)
Clement M. Bakkache (1928–1958)
Rabula Y. Bakkache (1958–1963)
Basil P. Habra (1963–1977)
Basil M. Daud (1977–1995)
Joseph Hannouche (1996–)

Armenian Catholic Bishops of Cairo

Barnabas Akchérian (1886–1898)
Boghos Sabbaghian (1901–1904)
Bedros Koyounian (1908–1911)
Hvohannes Couzian (1911–1933)
Hagop Nessimian (1933–1960)
Rafael Bayan (1960–1989)
Butrus Taza (1990–2003)
Kerikor A. Koussa (2003–)

Syrian Catholic Patriarchs of Antioch

Michel Daher (1802–1810)
Simon Zora (1814–1818)
Pierre Jarweh (1820–1852)
Antoine Semheri I (1853–1864)
Philippe Arkousse (1865–1873)
Georges Solhote (1874–1891)
Behnam Benni (1892–1897)
Ephreem Rahmani (1898–1929)
Gabriel Tappuni (1929–1968)
Antoine Hayek II (1968–)

Chaldean Catholic Patriarchs of Babylon

John VIII Hormez (1830–1838)
Nicolaos I (1840–1847)
Joseph VI Audo (1848–1878)

Elias XIII Abolyonan (1879–1894)
Joseph Emmanuel II (1900–1947)
Joseph VII Ghanima (1947–1958)
Paul II Cheikho (1958–1989)
Raphael I Bàdawid (1989–2003)
Emmanuel III Karim Delly (2004–)

The Episcopal Bishops in Egypt

Gwynne	1920–1946
Johnson Alan	1947–1952
Francis Johnson	1952–1958
Archeacon Ishaq Musaad	1958–1970
Kenneth Cragg	1970–1974
Ishaq Mussad	1974–1981
Gais Abdel Malik	1984–2000
Munir Anis	2000–

(From 1958–1976, the Diocese of Egypt was part of the Archbishopric of Jerusalem).

Presidents of the Middle East Council of Churches

1974	H.G. Bishop Samuel (Orient. Orth.)
1974	Rev. Dr. Hovannes Aharounian (Evang.)
1974	H.B. Patriarch Ignatios IV Hazim (Greek Orth.)
1981	H.H. Catholicos Karekin I (Orient. Orth.)
1985	H.G. Bishop Samir Kafity (Evang.)
1990	H.E. Patriarch Ignatius Zakka Iwas I (Orient. Orth.)
1990	H.G. Bishop Youssef al. Khoury (Catholic)
1992	H.B. Patriarch Jeanne Pierre XVIII Kasparian (Catholic)
1994	H.H. Pope Shenuda III (Orient. Orth.)
1994	H.H. Pope Parthenios III of Alexandria (Greek Orth.)
1994	H.B. Patriarch Michael Sabbah of Jerusalem (Catholic)
1994	Rev. Dr. Salim Sahiouny (Evang.)
1996	H.E. Metropolitan Chrysanthos of Cyprus (Greek Orth.)
2003	H.H. Pope Petros VII (Greek Orth.)
2003	H.B. Patriarch Irenaios I of Jerusalem (Greek Orth.)
2003	H.H. Pope Shenuda III (Orient. Orth.)
2003	Rev. Dr. Safwat al-Bayadi (Evang.)
2003	H.G. Bishop Yuhanna Qulta (Catholic)

Postscript: Multicultural and Ecumenical Spirituality in Egypt

For Christians and non-Christians alike, the sad fragmentation of the Church of Jesus Christ must evoke sadness and concern, especially in a non-Christian environment, be it secular or Islamic. Responsible churchmen have realized the discrepancy between the Lord's high-priestly prayer *ut unum omnes sint* and the twenty-first century realities. One answer to this embarrassment lies in a spiritual awakening. This has occurred among those who have turned away from property, prestige, and positions! The following survey of ecumenical relations in Egypt will inspire the present generation to discover in the wisdom of their fathers answers to the present religious predicaments.

The Emergence of Multicultural Monasticism in Egypt

It is noteworthy that certain places of solitude have often attracted men of prayer belonging to different ethnic origins and cultural backgrounds. This is true regarding the multicultural monastic life of the Greeks, Russians, Rumanians, and Bulgarians on Mount Athos. It is also the case of the first monastic settlements in the desert of Scetis, the Wadi al-Natrun between Cairo and Alexandria. Among the first monks were Maximus and Domitius, sons of the West-Roman Emperor Valentinian (364–375) who were instructed in the ascetic life by St. Macarius the Great. Bishop Palladius of Helenopolis (fourth century) mentioned in his *Historia Lauiaca* the Ethiopian robber Moses the Black, who had joined St. Isidore in the Cell of the Romans *(al-Baramus)* and who had suffered martyrdom during the Berber raid of 407. Other foreigners in the desert of Scetis were the Roman aristocrat Arsenius (376–449), the Roman historian John Cassianus (360–430), and his friend Germanus. Evagrius of Pontus (345–400) was a personal friend of St. Macarius. He had spent two years in Nitria and fourteen more years in the Cells *(Cellia)*. According to Coptic tradition, St. Ephraim the Syrian also visited St. Bishoi in the desert of Scetis.

In fact, the ecumenical and multicultural character of the ascetic life in the Western Desert had inspired several European ladies of distinction to assume the monastic apparel and join the desert fathers. Among the best known were Hilaria, the daughter of the Byzantine Emperor Zeno (479–491); Eugenia, the daughter of the Alexandrian Prefect Philippus; Apollonia, the daughter of the Roman Emperor Anthemius (467–472); and the noble ladies Euphrosyne, Theodora and Anastasia. This practice of the so-called women monks led the Church Fathers to issue the following canon at the Council of Gangra (fourth century): "If a woman, under the pretense of asceticism shall change her apparel and, instead of a woman's accustomed clothing, shall put on that of a man, let her be anathema."

Other early foreigners who visited the desert fathers were the Aquileian historian Rufinus (345–410), who was accompanied by the Roman Lady Melania. Also St. Jerome (348–430), after he had settled in Bethlehem in 386, visited the Egyptian desert fathers. The fame of the elders of Scetis spread to distant lands and attracted many pilgrims, even from Ireland and Spain. An Irish guidebook for travelers to the Holy Land of Scetis is still preserved in the Bibliothèque Nationale in Paris.[96]

Although the Third Ecumenical Council of Ephesus in 431 had condemned the Nestorians for their Christological heresy, Nestorian monks continued to visit the Egyptian desert fathers. St. Eugenius, the father of Nestorian-Mesopotamian monasticism, visited the Scetis with his disciples. Other Nestorian monks like Rabban Sari, Abraham of Kashkar (492–586), Rabban Bar 'Idta, and Rabban Haia of Kashkar learned their ascetic practices from the Egyptian fathers. The example of the Coptic ascetes inspired such well-known Nestorian Church Fathers as Rabban Yunan of Anbar and Mar Yuhannan of Qanqal.[97]

The Antiochene-Alexandrian Connections

The traditional theological consensus between the miaphysitic patriarchates of Antioch and Alexandria is well documented on the famous tenth-century sanctuary doors of the old Church of the Holy Virgin in the Monastery of the Syrians in the Wadi al-Natrun. The Alexandrian Saints Mark and Diocorous and the Antiochene Saints Ignatius and Severus I are equally presented among the Church Fathers in the upper row of the panels. The balance of these Church Fathers demonstrates the intimate relationship of the two miaphysitic patriarchates. The murals painted on the semi-domes of the choir in the Church of the Holy Virgin, the Annunciation, and the Nativity of Christ, as well as the Dormition of the Holy Virgin, were the work of tenth-century Syrian artists, a period in which Moses of Nisibis served as abbot of the Monastery of the Syrians.

Already in the seventh century, a Syrian colony of monks had settled at the Ennaton Monastery, seven miles west of Alexandria where Thomas of Harkel and Paul of Tella had revised Syriac biblical texts. Two centuries later, toward the ninth century, Matthew and Abraham of Tekrit occupied the Theotokos Monastery of St. Bishoi, which Marutha ibn Habib, a Syrian businessman residing in Cairo, had acquired for the Syrian monks. The influence of the Syrians in the life of the Coptic Church during the tenth century is undoubtedly best illustrated by the nomination, election, and consecration of the Syrian businessman Abraham ibn Zar'ah (975–978) as sixty-second successor to the Evangelist St. Mark, an event that was celebrated in the historic Coptic church of the Syrian saints Sergius and Bacchus in Old Cairo. At least until the fourteenth century, Syrian monks used to play an important role in the desert of Scetis, where more than sixty monks inhabited the Syrian monastery.

The Expansion of Multicultural Monasticism in Scetis

During the Fatimid era (tenth–twelfth centuries) Syrians and Armenians settled in Egypt. St. Manakis, wearer of a hairshirt, was the first Armenian monk to move to the desert of Scetis in the tenth century. Other Armenians followed him. Until the fourteenth century at least an Armenian monastery existed in the Western desert which was situated between the Monastery of St. Bishoi and that of St. John Colobus. According to al-Maqrizi, by the fifteenth century the Armenian monastery had fallen into ruin.

In the latter part of the eleventh century, the Armenian Catholicus St.Vahran, known as St. Gregory II, had visited the monks in the desert of Scetis. In honor of the Armenian hierarch's visit, Coptic, Ethiopian, Nubian, Syrian came together for multicultural composition of desert monasticism in the Scetis.

Apart from the Ethiopian robber St. Moses the Black (fourth century), who had settled in the Cell of the Romans, by the ninth century other Ethiopian monks had joined the Egyptian desert fathers. The Ethiopian Synaxar (*Hamlé* 19) mentions the Abbot Andrew, who had received the monastic habit from St. John Kame of the Monastery of the Syrians (ninth century). By the eleventh century, Ethiopian monks had settled in the Cell of Pehout in the *laura* of the Monastery of St. John Colobus near the Monastery of St. Bishoi. Undoubtedly, this cell used to serve as a nucleus for the Ethiopian Monastery of St. Elias. Both, the *Vita* of St. Takla Haymanot and the Ethiopian Synaxar (*Nahassé* 14) record the presence of St. Takla Haymanot (thirteenth century), the national saint of Ethiopia, in the desert of Scetis. On the occasion of the visit of Pope Benjamin II (1327–1339) to the Desert Fathers of Scetis, the Ethiopians had joined the Copts in the liturgical celebrations in the Monastery of St. John Colobus. The fourteenth-century German pilgrim Ludoloph of Suchem mentions in his travel-account the Syrian, Ethiopian, and Nubian monks who followed the monastic rules of Sts. Antony and Macarius. A text of the beginning of the fifteenth century clearly states that Ethiopians still inhabited the Monastery of St. Elias. However, a few years later they were forced to abandon their monastery which had fallen victim to ants. Thus they moved first to the smaller Theotokos Monastery of St. John Colobus.

Although the Nubians had retained their ecclesiastical identity in the Desert of Scetis, it is likely that they lived together with the Ethiopians since there is no mention of a separate Nubian monastery. On the occasion of the visit of the Armenian Catholicus St. Vaharan in 1088 they are mentioned as a separate group. This fact is also supported by the Nubian marble tray (seventy-two centimeters in diameter) which is kept in the museum of the Monastery of the Syrians. The long Nubian inscription on the base of the tray includes intercessions for the Nubian King George who ruled from 1130–1158.[99] As the Ethiopian monks migrated to the Monastery of the Syrians between 1419 and 1449 they must have taken the marble tray along with them.

Although the Abbasid caliphs of Baghdad had regarded the Nestorians as being the "only true Christians," the medieval Copts had condemned them on account of their Christological heresies and had scorned them as being "the new Jews." They were not represented in the Western desert. Their monastery was situated in al-Adawiya in the Nile Valley south of Cairo.

Nevertheless, during some three hundred years, from the twelfth to the fifteenth centuries, the multicultural composition of the desert fathers in the Scetis must be seen as a most remarkable event in the history of the ecumenical movement. Although they all shared the same miaphysitic Christology based upon the confession of St. Cyril of Alexandria, their ethnic, cultural, and linguistic differences were extraordinary. There were the Indo-Germanic Armenians of the Caucasus regions. The southernmost representatives were the Ethiopians belonging to the Kushitic or Nilotic tribes, speaking Tigrinya or the south-Ethiopian Amharic. Then Nilosahraric Nubians using their Shari languages were the spiritual heirs of the legendary King Melchior. The Syrian monks speaking their West-Aramaic dialect considered themselves culturally and linguistically related to the biblical traditions, to the language and culture of Christ and the Apostles. Finally, there were the Copts, sons of the Pharaohs and great-grandchildren of Noah (Genesis 10.6). Since the eleventh century the Coptic-Bohairic dialect had become the official liturgical language. For their daily communications, Arabic would have served as their lingua franca. In their ecumenical services, and the reading of the Holy Scriptures, the desert fathers would have used the Greek language, since this was the language in which the New Testament was written originally. The fourteenth-century Coptic-Arabic-Greek Holy Week Lectionary of the Monastery of St. Macarius testifies to the use of the Greek text for multicultural Divine Services.[100]

About Multicultural Services in the Scetis

During the fourteenth century, the multicultural, ecumenical life in the desert of Scetis had reached its climax as well as the beginning of its regrettable decline. In addition to the Ethiopians, Nubians, Armenians, and Syrians, the Copts still inhabited six monasteries. The terrible persecutions of the Christians by the Bahri-Mamluks, especially under Sultan al-Malik al-Nasir Muhammad (1320–21) and the Black Death, the bubonic plague which ravaged Egypt during 1347 and 1348, led the desert fathers of the various communities to "move together." Therefore, the multicultural ecumenicity should also be seen as a response to their needs for survival. A significant document of this "ecumenical togetherness" is the fourteenth century Polyglot-Psalter of the Monastery of St. Macarius in which the Psalms appear in five languages from left to right in Ge'ez, Syriac, Bohairic, Arabic, and Armenian. The marginal notes were written in Syriac which indicates that the "project" may have originated among the Syrian monks.[101] There is no doubt, that since the eleventh century Syrian monks also resided in the Monastery of St. Macarius. On account of the threatening situations in the monasteries, Pope Benjamin II visited the desert of

Scetis in 1330. It is most likely, that the fourteenth-century trilingual Holy Week Lectionary, as well as the Greek-Arabic Euchologion—which even mentions Pope Benjamin—were used for the multicultural Divine Services at the Monastery of St. Macarius and that of St. John Colobus.

The Period of the Ecumenical Dispersion

The dissolution of the southern Christian Kingdom of Alodia (Nubia) at the beginning of the sixteenth century led to the collapse of the Nubian monastic community in Scetis. During the final years of the fifteenth century the Armenian monastery had also fallen into ruin. Only the Ethiopians and Syrians continued to reside within the remaining four Coptic monasteries. For the Syrian monks, the fifteenth century had turned out to be "the golden age," Syrian writers like Daud ibn Butrus, Habib, and Garir of Tekrit had significantly enriched the Syrian theological literature. At the beginning of the sixteenth century, Pope Gabriel VII (1526–1569) could still commission monks from the Syrian Monastery to assist in the reconstruction of the two devastated Red Sea Monasteries of St. Antony and St. Paul the Theban. Yet the decline could not be stopped. In 1634, the Evangelical Lutheran lay-missionary Peter Heyling of Lübeck was the last person to record the presence of Syrian monks in the Monastery of the Syrians. On the other hand, Ethiopian monks continued to reside in Coptic monasteries. In the sixteenth and the beginning of the seventeenth century, a significant Ethiopian community existed in the Monastery of St. Antony. Throughout the Middle Ages until the twentieth century larger and smaller groups of Ethiopian monks resided in the Monastery of the Holy Virgin al-Muharraq in the Nile Valley. During the first half of the nineteenth century a significant Ethiopian group of monks had separate rooms in the Monastery of the Syrians. Individual Ethiopian monks have also continued to live as itinerants or hermits in the Nile Valley or in the desert monasteries.

Today, the patriarchal Monastery of St. Bishoi serves as an ecumenical center of the Coptic Church, thereby continuing the ecclesiastical tradition of the desert fathers which had its zenith in the fourteenth century.

Annotations on the Text

Some of the material presented in this volume has appeared in one form or another in some of my previous publications. Wherever necessary, corrections and additions to the original texts have been made.

1. Parts of "Egyptian Christians as Heirs of the Pharaonic Heritage" have appeared in *Coptologia* 19, 2003, 50–62.
2. Parts of "Egyptian Christians as Citizens of an Islamic Society in the Middle Ages" In *Christian Egypt: Faith and Life* (Cairo: The American University in Cairo Press, 1970), 342–65.
3. "A Historical Note" in *Christian Egypt: Ancient and Modern* (Cairo: The American University in Cairo Press, 1977), 2–7.
   "Issues of Coptic Orthodox Inculturation . . ." in *Coptic Church Review* XVIII/3 (1997): 67–77.
   "The Armenian Orthodox Church in Egypt" in *Christian Egypt: Ancient and Modern* (Cairo: The American University in Cairo Press, 1977), 552–55.
   "The Syrian Orthodox Church in Egypt" in *Christian Egypt: Ancient and Modern* (Cairo: The American University in Cairo Press, 1977), 557.
   "The Mission of Peter Heyling of Lübeck" in *Ostkirchliche Studien* XIV (1965): 305–26.
4. YMCA and YWCA in *Christian Egypt: Ancient and Modern* (Cairo: The American University in Cairo Press, 1977), 586, 587.
5. "Christian Feasts and Fasts" in Christian Egypt: Ancient and Modern (Cairo: The American University in Cairo Press, 1977), 131–37.

"Postscript" in *Coptic Church Review* 20/4 (1999): 128–34.

Notes

1. Lawrence Durrell, *The Alexandria Quartet: Justine, Balthazar, Mountolive, Clea.* (London: Faber and Faber, 1968).
2. Socrates. H.E. *Patrologia Latina*, ed. J.P. Migne (Paris, 1844–1864), trans. A.C. Zenos (New York: The Christian Literature, 1890) Book V, Chapter XVII.
3. Johannes Leipoldt, *Sinuthii Archimandrite Vita Et Opera Omina*, vol. 3 (CSCO 42 [Copt. 2]; Paris 1908), p. 105, lines 27–28, p. 106, lines 1–5.
4. Alfred J. Butler. T*he Churches and Monasteries of Egypt and Some Neighboring Countries*, ed. and trans. B.T.A. Evetts. Oxford: Clarendon Press, 1895.
5. Sawtrus ibn al-Muqaffa', *History of the Patriarchs of the Egyptian Church*, trans. Yassa 'Abd al-Masih and O.H.E. Burmester. Cairo, 1943) vol. 2, part 2, p. 113.
6. C.S. Sonnim. *Travels in Upper and Lower Egypt.* (Farmboroush, England: Gregg, 1972) 368.
7. *Patrologia Latina*, ed. J.-P. Migne (Paris, 1844–1864).
8. "History of Joseph the Carpenter" in *Ante-Niccene Fathers*, vol. VIII, eds. A. Roberts and J. Donaldson. (T&T Clark: Edinburgh), line 26.
9. Edward W. Lane, *The Manners and Customs of the Modern Egyptians* (London: JM Dent, 1908): 67.
10. Winifred S. Blackman, *The Fellahin of Upper Egypt* (London: Cassells, 1968; reprint of 1927 edition): 121.
11. Herodotus. Histories: *The Ancient Empires of the East* II (trans. and ed. by A.H. Sayce, 1895): 85.
12. Henry Habib Ayrout, *The Egyptian Peasant*, trans. John A Williams (Boston: Beacon Press, 1966): 133.
13. The most recent informative study on present Christian-Islamic relations in Egypt is Cornelis Hulsman, *The Freedom of Christians in Egypt: A new approach to reporting religious freedom in an Islamic Context. . . .* (Aachen: Missio, 2007).
    This manuscript has been extremely well received in discussions with various experts. This study is an elaboration of: Cornelis Hulsman, *Persecuted Christians? Case Study of Egypt* (Aachen: Missio, 2001); *Arab-West Report*, 50A, art. 30, 2002;

Religious News Service from the Arab World, "Christians in Egypt: The impact of Islamic resurgence," December 27, 2002.

14. The exceptions are the fourteenth-century theologians Abu'l-Barakat and Huhanna ibn abi Zaharya Ibn Sabba. See G. Graf, Geschichte der christlichen arabischen Literature. II, III. Città del Vaticano 1947.
15. Evetts, B.T.A., Hist Patr. In Patrologia Orientalis, I, V, X. Burmester, O.H.E. KHS-Yassa 'Abd al-Masih, Hist. Patr. II, I. Burmester, O.H.E. KHS, Atiya A.S., Yassa 'Abd al-Masih, Hist. Patr. II, II & III.
16. B.T.A. Evetts (ed. and trans.), The Churches and Monasteries of Egypt and Some Neighbouring Countries Attributed to Abu Saleh the Armenian (Oxford: Clarendon Press 1895).
17. Wüstenfeld, F., Maqrizi's Geschichte der Copten. Göttingen 1845. Also as addendum in Evetts, op. cit., and S.S. Malan, A Short History of the Copts and of Their Church (London, 1873).
18. The dhimmis are the non-Muslim residents in Muslim territory who had to pay a personal tax (jizya) in recognition for their protection by the state.
19. G.W., ""Kibt," Encylopedia of Islam, "Kibt," (Leiden: Brill) vol. 2, 1927, pp. 990–1003; M. Hamidullah, Muslim Conduct of the State (Hyderabad-Deccan, 1941)—see his bibliography pp. 191–203; also, W. Shedd, Islam and the Oriental Churches (Philadelphia, 1904).
20. Basset, René, "Le Synaxaire Arabe Jacobite," Patr. Orient. I, III, XVI, XVIL.
21. The Synaxarium was compiled by Peter, Bishop of Malig, between the last quarter of the twelfth and the first half of the thirteenth century. O.H.E. KHS-Burmester, "On the date and authorship of the Arabic Synaxarium of the Coptic Church," Journal of Theological Studies XXXVIII, 240–53.
22. The Qur'an, 2:62.
23. P.M. Fraser, "Arab Conquest of Egypt," in: *Coptic Encyclopedia*, Macmillan Publishing Company, 1991, vol 1, pp. 183–89.
24. Alfred Butler, *The Churches and Monasteries of Egypt and Some Neighbouring Countries*, ed. and trans. B.T.A. Evetts. (Oxford: Clarendon Press, 1895).
25. Proverbs 3:11.
26. Sawirus ibn al-Muqaffa'. *History of the Patriarchs of the Egyptian Church*. vol. 2, Part 1.
27. Sawirus ibn al-Muqaffa'. *History of the Patriarchs of the Egyptian Church*, vol. 2. See also the Coptic Encyclopedia, pp. 1410–12.
28. *The Chronicle of John, Coptic Bishop of Niku*, trans. Robert Henry Charles. Amsterdam: Philo Press, 1916), CXX 37, p. 195.

29. St. John of Damascus; *De Haeresibus*. Patrologia Graeca, ed. J.P. Migne. vol XCIV, pp. 764–73 and D.J. Sahas. *John of Damascus on Islam* (Leiden: Brill, 1972).
30. Sawiris, Vol. 2, Part I.
31. Sawiris ibn Muqaffa, *History of the Patriarchs*, vol. I, p. 497.
32. Sawiris ibn Muqaffa, *History of the Patriarchs*, vol. II, part II, p. 136.
33. Sawiris ibn Muqaffa, *History of the Patriarchs*, vol. II, part II, p. 144.
34. Eusebius HE VII, 7 see Davis, op. cit., 27.
35. Epipnanius. *Panarion*, trans. F. Williams. Nas Hammadi Studies 36. (Lieden: E.J. Brill, 1994), Line 72.
36. Eusebius of Caesarea. *Historia Ecclesiastica*, trans. G.A. Williamson. (New York: Penguin, 1965), Book VI. Chapter 46, Line 2.
37. On the island of Iona, Inner Hebrides, St. Columban founded the monastery in 563. It became the most famous center of Celtic Christianity.
38. Glastonbury, Somerset, according to twelfth-century tradition it was the site of King Arthur's tomb and of the wattle-church by St. Joseph of Arimathea.
39. Toulon, fortress on the Mediterranean where Napoleon organized his Egyptian campaign.
40. Wolfram Reiss, *Erneuerung in der koptischen Kirche-Orthodoxen Kirche. Die Geschichte der Koptisch-orthodoxen Sonntagsschulbewegung* (Hamburg, 1998).
41. I received this text from Bishop Tawfilus of the Dair al-Surian in 1959.
42. According to the seventh canon of St. Athanasius, the altar "be it of wood or stone, is no more mortal as to its former substances, but liveth and is spiritual, for the living God standeth thereon."
43. Numerous monks had left the monastery for the eremitical life in the cave, so also Father Antonius al-Suriani, the present Pope Shenuda III. In April 1965 Pope Cyril VI issued an order for itinerant monks to return to their monasteries.
44. For a detailed description of these monasteries see O. Meinardus, *Two Thousand Years of Coptic Christianity* (Cairo: The American University Press, 2002).
45. O. Meinardus, "Die Eremiten des Wadi al-Rayan 2004" Kemet 4, 2004.
46. O. Meinardus, "Marks of Identification: Tattoo and Name," in *Christian Egypt Faith and Life* (Cairo: French Institute of Oriental Archaeology, 1970): 1–14.
47. O. Meinardus, *Christian Egypt Ancient and Modern*. (Cairo: French Institute of Oriental Archaeology, 1965: 107.
48. Shenouda III, "The Policy of the Coptic Church in the Countries of the Emigration," El Keraza IV/6 (1712/1995): 12–13.
49. Copts use religious pictures not only at home, but in wallets, in books, glued as small stickers to all kinds of objects.

50. Ishak, F.M. "The Miraculous Appearance of the Lord," *Coptologia* 10 (1989): 15–16.
51. "Les Icônes Miraculeuses: une example récente," *Le Monde Copte* 19 1(1991): 107–10.
52. "Weeping Jesus goes on display in Bellaire," *The Houston Post*, Jan. 7 (1992); "Jesus Wept." Houston Chronicle, Jan. 11 (1992). See also Morgan David, "Sallman's Head of Christ, the history of an image," *Christian Century*, Oct. 7 (1992): 868–70.
53. Ragnhild Bjerre Finnestad, "Image as Messenger of Coptic Identity," in *Dance, Music, Art and Religion Symposium, Abo, Finland*, August 16/18, 1994, Stockholm: 101.
54. O. Meinardus, "Von der Mariophanie zum Ganadenbild. Zur ikonographischen Entwicklung der Gnadenbilder von Zeitûn und Ard Babadeblu," *Ostkirchliche Studien* 39/4 (1990): 289–99.
55. O. Meinardus, "Carlo Dolcis 'Mater Dolorosa' in der koptischen Mariologie," Orientalia Suecana 41/42 (1992/1993): 155–65.
56. Gregorius, "The Recognition of the Sacraments of Other Churches by the Coptic Orthodox Church," *Coptologia* XI (1990): 57ff.
57. *St. George Youth Magazine*, NSW, Australia, vols. II (1992).
58. Wakin, Edward, *A Lonely Minority. The Modern Story of Egypt's Copts* (New York, 2000): 160.
59. Ibid.
60. Ibid.
61. In 1970 Father Ghobrial Amin was sent to Jersey City, Father Bishoi Kamel came to Los Angeles in 1969.
62. Fayek M. Ishak, "Immigrant Copts Striking Roots in the Lands of the Diaspora," *Coptologia* X (1989).
63. For a detailed presentation of the Council of Chalcedon and its effects on the parties involved, see Stephen J. Davis, *The Early Coptic Papacy: The Egyptian Church and Its Leadership in Late Antiquity* (Cairo: The American University Press, 2004).
64. It was Pope Leo of Rome who had labeled the second council of Ephesus (449) a *latrocinium*, a Council of Robbers.
65. From the 1971 meeting.
66. The seven ecumenical councils: Nicea (325), Constantinople (381), Ephesus (431), Chalcedon (451), Constantinople II (553), Constantinople III (680), Nicea II (787).
67. Dr. Karam Khella.
68. *Hemerologion ekklesias Alexandreias*, 2004.
69. The original name of Alexandria.
70. Fustat.

71. The Nile Delta.
72. The Nobatai, Makourians, and Bal an-Hmoou were Nubian miaphysite Christians.
73. The Coptic Catholic Patriarch of Alexandria keeps its own coptic canon law.
74. *Exultate Deo* (1439), *Cantate Domino* 1442, and *Multa et admirabilia* (1444).
75. The Christological agreement was based upon the cyrilian formula: "*mia physis (or mia hypothasis) tou theou logou sesarkomeon*," the one physis (nature) of God's Word Incarnate.
76. The stoics conceived a middle place of enlightenment which they called "empyrosis."
77. *Azyme*, the Jewish Passover cake of unleavened bread.
78. The Annuciation to Joachim and Anne (Misra 7, August 13)
The Nativity of the Holy Virgin (Bashons 1, May 9)
The Presentation of Holy Virgin in the Temple (Kihak 3, December 12).
The Annunciation to the Holy Virgin (Baramhat 29, April 7).
The Dormition of the Holy Virgin (Tuba 21, January 29).
The Assumption of the Holy Virgin (Misra 16, August 22).
The Mariophany of Zeitun (Baramhat 24, 1684, April 2).
The twenty-second day of each Coptic month.
79. The Immaculate Conception should not be confused with the Virginal Conception and the Virgin Birth which asserts Mary's perpetual virginity, a doctrine also held by the Copts.
80. The devotion to the Sacred Heart of Jesus follows a revelation of Christ to the French nun Marguerite Marie Alacoque (1647–690). The devotion to the Pure Heart of Mary, first fostered by St. John Eudes (seventeenth century), was authorized in 1857 by Pope Pius IX. Pope Pius XII consecrated the world to the Immaculate Heart of Mary in 1942, a feast to be observed on August 22, the octave of the Assumption.
81. Dom Cuthbert Butler, *The Vatican Council*, London 1930, 2 vols. Vatican I, Session IV, Const. de Ecclesia Christi, c. iv.
82. See Meinardes, "Peter Heyling, History and Legend," *Ostkirchliche Studient* 14 (1965): 305–26. Ludolf Hiob. *Historia Agthiopica*, trans J.P. Gent. (London, 1884).
83. Julius Richter. *A History of Protestant Missions in the Near East*. (New York: Fleming N. Revell, 1910), p. 92–93.
84. For further information see Beth Prim Howell, *Lady on a Donkey* (New York: E.P. Dutton & Co.1960), and Lester Sumrall, *Lillian Trasher, The Nile Mother*, (Springfield: Gospel Publishing House, 1951).
85. Ruz al-Yusuf, March 8–14, 2003 with review in *Arab-West Report*, 2003, 10, 38.
86. Ouverture du dialogue théologique entre d'Eglise Copte Orthodox et l'Eglise Copte Évangelique, *PPC* 39 (1989): 334–36.

87. In view of this agreement one wonders why Protestant persons applying to marry an Orthodox Copt in a Coptic Orthodox Church must be rebaptized.
88. According to Coptic tradition, the apostles had appointed bishops as their successors who were in possession of special divine grace enabling them to transmit and interpret without error the teachings of the apostles. Irenaeus, Tertullian and Hippolytus are the earliest witnesses to the 'Apostolic Succession.'
89. The seven sacraments are: Baptism (John 3:5); Chrismation (1 John 2:20); Oblation (Matthew 26:26–29); Ordination of priests (John 20:21–23); Confession (Matthew 18:18); Matrimony (Matthew 19:4–6); and Unction (James 5:14).
90. O. Meinardus, *Christian Egypt: Faith and Life*, op. cit.: 52–89.
91. For a breakdown of the various groups of saints, see O. Meinardus, *Christian Egypt: Ancient and Modern*, op. cit., 80.
92. Cyril IV is reported to have said: "Behold, those wooden pictures you used to honor and even worship can neither avail nor harm, God alone shuld be adored" see Edith L. Butcher, *The Story of the Church of Egypt* (London, 1897).
93. Hanna F. Wissa, *Assiout: the Saga of an Egyptian Family* (Lewes, Sussex: The Book Guild, 1994): 109.
94. A feddan is a little less than an acre.
95. Henry Habib Ayrout, *The Egyptian Peasant*, trans. John A. Williams (Boston: Beacon Press, 1963).
96. De Lacy O'Leary, *The Saints of Egypt* (London, 1937): 27.
97. O. Meinardus, "The Nestorians in Egypt," Oriens Christimas 51 (1967): 122.
98. O. Meinardus, *Monks and Monasteries of the Egyptian Desert* (Cairo, 1961): 241ff.
99. O. Meinardus, "Die christichen Königreiche Nubiens," Kemet 4 (1996).
100. O.H.E. Khs-Burmester, "A Coptic-Greek-Arabic Holy Week Lectinary," BSAC 16, (1961–62).
101. This psalter (235 fols.) was acquired in 1635 from the Monastery of St. Macarius by the Capuchin monk Agathangelus de Vendôme for Nicolas C.F. Peiresc of Paris. Twice during its transport the manuscript was lost. Finally, Giovanni Lascaris saved the precious document and presented it to Francesco Cardinal Barberini. It is now in the Biblioteca Apostolica Vaticana, Rome.

Bibliography

Annuaire Catholique d'Egypte, Cairo 2004.

Ayrout, Henry Habib. 1963. *The Egyptian Peasant*, trans. John A Williams. Boston: Beacon Press.

Coptic Diary 2004, 1720–1721 AM. Kogarah, NSW, C.O.P.T., Australia

Davis, Stephen, J. 2004. *The Early Coptic Papacy: The Egyptian Church and Its Leadership in Late Antiquity*. Cairo: The American University in Cairo Press.

Elder, Earl E. 1958. *Vindicating a Vision: The Story of the American Mission in Egypt 1854–1954*. Philadelphia: Board of Foreign Missions of the United Presbyterian Church of North America.

Evetts, B.T.A. 1895. *The Churches and Monasteries of Egypt and Some Neighbouring Countries Attributed to Abu Saleh the Armenian*. Oxford: Clarendon Press.

Gabra, Gawdat. 2002. *Coptic Monasteries: Egypt's Monastic Art and Architecture*. Cairo: The American University in Cairo Press.

Gerhards, Albert and Heinzgerd Brakman. 1994. *Die Koptische Kirche. Einführung in das ägyptische Christentum*. Stuttgart.

Hady, Amal Abdel (ed.). 2003. *Empowerment: From Theory into Practice CEOSS Experience in the Area of the Eradication of Female Genital Cutting*. Cairo.

Hanna, Milad. 2001. *Acceptance of the Other*. Cairo.

Hasan, S.S. 2003. *Christians Versus Muslims in Modern Egypt. The Century-long Struggle for Coptic Equality*. Oxford: Oxford University Press.

Hemerologion Ekklesias Alexandreias. 2004. Alexandria.

Hulsman, Cornelis. 2007. *The Freedom of Christians in Egypt*. Missio.

Meinardus, Otto F.A. 1962. *Atlas of Christian Sites in Egypt*. Cairo: French Institute of Oriental Archaeology.

———. 1965 and 1977. *Christian Egypt Ancient and Modern*. Cairo: French Institute of Oriental Archaeology.

———. 1970. *Christian Egypt Faith and Life*. Cairo: French Institute of Oriental Archaeology.

———. 1999. *Two Thousand Years of Coptic Christianity*. Cairo: The American University in Cairo Press.

———. 2002. *Coptic Saints and Pilgrimages*. Cairo: The American University in Cairo Press.

Panzer, Regina. 1997. *Identität und Geschichtsbewußtsein. Griechisch-orthodoxe Christen in Vorderen Orient zwischen Byzant und Arabertum*. Hamburg.

Patrick, T.H. 1996. *Traditional Egyptian Christianity: A History of the Coptic Orthodox Church*. Greensboro, NC: Fisher Park Press.

Petry, Carl F. 1991. "Copts in late medieval Egypt," *Coptic Encyclopedia*. II, 618–35. New York: McMillan.

Pink, Johanna. 2003. *Neue Religionsgemeinschaften in Ägytpen. Minderheiten im Spannungsfeld von Glaubensfreiheit, öffentlicher Ordnung und Islam*. Würzburg.

Reiss, Wolfram. 1998. *Erneuerung in der Koptisch-Orthodoxen Kirche. Die Geschichte der Koptisch-orthodoxen Sonntagsschulbewegung*. Hamburg.

Roncaglia, Martiniano. 1954. *St. Francis of Assisi and the Middle East. Cairo Histoire de l'Eglise Copte*. 3 vols. Beirut, 1966–1969. Sawtrus ibn al-Muqaffa'. 1943. *History of the Patriarchs of the Egyptian Church*, trans. Yassa 'Abd al-Masih and O.H.E. Burmester. Cairo, vol. 2, part 2, p. 113.

Strothmann, R. 1932. *Die Koptische Kirche in der Neuzeit*. Tübingen.

Timm, Stefan. 1984. *Das christlich-koptische Ägypten in arabischer Zeit. Beihefte zum Tübimger Atlas des Vorderen Orients* (TAVO). Vols 1–6. Wiesbaden.

Van Doorn-Harder, Nelly, and Kari Vogt (eds.). 1997. *Between Desert and City: The Coptic Orthodox Church Today*. Oslo: Wipf and Stock.

Virtue, David W. 1996. *A Vision of Hope*. Oxford.

Wakin, Edward. 1963. *A Lonely Minority: The Modern Story of Egypt's Copts*. New York: Backprint.com.

Watson, John H. 2000. *Among the Copts*. Brighton, Sussex.

Winkler, Dietmar W. 1997. *Koptische Kirche und Reichskirche. Altes Schisma und neuer Dialog*. Innsbruck.

Wissa, Hanna F. 1994. *Assiout: The Saga of an Egyptian Family*. Lewes, Sussex: The Book Guild.

Index